WHITENESS

The MIT Press Essential Knowledge Series

A complete list of books in this series can be found online at
https://mitpress.mit.edu/books/series/mit-press-essential-knowledge-series.

WHITENESS

MARTIN LUND

The MIT Press | Cambridge, Massachusetts | London, England

The MIT Press would like to thank the anonymous peer reviewers who provided comments on drafts of this book. The generous work of academic experts is essential for establishing the authority and quality of our publications. We acknowledge with gratitude the contributions of these otherwise uncredited readers.

This book was set in Chaparral Pro by New Best-set Typesetters Ltd. Printed and bound in the United States of America.

Library of Congress Cataloging-in-Publication Data

Names: Lund, Martin, 1984- author.
Title: Whiteness / Martin Lund.
Description: Cambridge, Massachusetts : The MIT Press, [2022] | Series: The MIT press essential knowledge series | Includes bibliographical references and index.
Identifiers: LCCN 2021057610 | ISBN 9780262544191 (paperback)
Subjects: LCSH: White people—Race identity. | White people—Social conditions.
Classification: LCC HT1575 .L86 2022 | DDC 305.809—dc23/eng/20220207
LC record available at https://lccn.loc.gov/2021057610

10 9 8 7 6 5 4 3 2 1

Similarly, although I look at other national contexts, I use more examples from the United States and Sweden than anywhere else. Not only are these countries the most familiar to me, but they differ in their public images and relations to race. US public discourse consistently takes race into account, and the United States is internationally viewed as a racist country. Sweden, on the other hand, is self-positioned as color-blind, has largely discarded the term "race," and is viewed internationally as progressive and equal. These differences make for fruitful comparisons. Yet it is important to remember that I am speaking about two different national formations of whiteness.

Since this book is intended to introduce a topic too complex to easily summarize or present in a neat way, I concentrate on the tip of the proverbial iceberg with the aim of making whiteness more legible to more people. The introduction genre has limits and necessitates a limited presentation of any topic. I've written this book half expecting to fail; these few pages cannot account for all the ways whiteness has been and continues to be constructed, lived, and enforced, nor can they satisfy every expectation of an introduction to whiteness. My hope is that whatever my failures may be, they aren't harmful.

The more the picture I'm outlining comes into focus, the clearer it will become that I offer only a sketch. *Whiteness* should thus be viewed as a starting point, not a comprehensive accounting of everything whiteness is, has been, and will be. For accessibility, I have opted wherever possible to cite more widely available sources in the body of the text. Scholarly monographs and articles can add much to this discussion, but specialized books are often expensive, and academic articles tend to be behind a paywall and prohibitively priced. Readers who want to continue learning about whiteness, its roots and effects, and the damage it can do to both those who aren't granted its privileges and those who are will find some suggestions for further reading at the end of the book.

Finally, my aim is not to level moral accusations when I speak about "white people"; the impetus is not to foster a "hatred of whites" or construct an argument in favor of so-called reverse racism. The point of looking critically at whiteness as a system or structure is not to paint white people as hateful monsters but rather to highlight patterns that have been in place since long before I or anybody reading this book were born, and that in all likelihood will remain long after we're dead, so as to help issue a necessary challenge.

Briefly about the Author

All scholarship is political. It is important to not get lost in the myth that science is somehow above the fray and neutral. Every scholar writes from a sociocultural subject position and with a certain perspective, informed by previous experiences and prior knowledges. I therefore want to attempt, briefly, to lay out where I'm speaking from.

When I write that it's impossible to stand to the side of whiteness and structural racism, I include myself among those caught inside a structure not of my own making. I am a white, cisgender, heterosexual, able-bodied, neurotypical, and fairly young man with stable employment in the professional class. I am, in short, privileged by many of the structures that shape life in my native Sweden, where I live and work at a state-funded university. And I'm privileged in the United States from the moment I deplane, whether I've come for a brief visit—which I did annually before the pandemic, not least to see my wife's family—or to stay for years, as I did for three years in New York City for a research project funded by the Swedish Research Council.

In the structural sense of the word, I am also racist; it's not my choice, but it's how I was raised. Not by my mother. Not by my brothers. Not intentionally. I grew up in a society permeated with racism in the things I watched and listened to, in the things I read, in my schooling—first in the mostly white village where I grew up, then at a mostly white high school in a then mostly white city, and thereafter at a mostly white department of religious studies at Lund University, all in southern Sweden—and so on. I could go through my undergraduate courses in religious studies and begin doctoral work in Jewish studies without ever encountering critical discussions of whiteness. My life until that point had been one of white segregation, with few exceptions, or nearly a textbook example of socialization into a white habitus. Because I have learned to view the world and move within it according to certain frameworks, it's unsurprising that I have said and done racist things, and that I will continue to do so. For much of my life, while I styled myself as nonracist and opposed explicit interpersonal racism, I remained unaware of how deeply favored I was in my every endeavor through no work of my own. For much of my life, I've let a racist structure stand unaddressed and unopposed.

I am working at being more aware of the harms I do, and to make them fewer and further between. I am working to address and oppose the racism that is everywhere around me. I can never be not racist, but I'm trying nevertheless to be antiracist. I'm trying with my teaching, what I choose to support and consume, where I spend or donate my money, who I vote for and support, and with works like this book, through my writing. I don't write this because I feel like I deserve a medal or want to style myself as "one of the good ones." I don't and I'm not. I wouldn't have been able to make these changes if someone else hadn't pointed me in the direction of a critique of whiteness. My hope is that *Whiteness* can help others to undertake the same work and follow it, wherever it may lead.

WHITENESS AND ITS
DISCONTENTS

The socially constructed phenomenon some of us call whiteness emerges, ultimately, from a paradox: whiteness doesn't exist in any palpable way identifiable across history and space, and yet the meanings attached to it have real effects. This chapter will begin by trying to clarify how that might be and expand on the definition above: *whiteness is a racial formation that functions as a system of social control.* This definition acknowledges that race or whiteness are never stable or finished, but rather are (re) produced through a contingent and ongoing so-called racial formation. Whiteness in this definition is both constituted by and constitutive of other social and cultural hierarchies—for example, class, gender, sexuality, and nationality—and it is simultaneously both a product and producer of power and privilege.

A consequence of this paradoxical duality is that whiteness is a frustratingly protean phenomenon, largely to the social, political, and economic benefit of those of us who are socially understood or believe ourselves to be white. Whiteness takes on different shapes and definitions depending on where we look, diachronically over time and synchronically across space. Although there are many similarities, whiteness today looks and works differently in the United States than in Sweden, Brazil, or South Africa. It might even be possible to talk about multiple "whitenesses" since there are many different meanings attached to what it means to be (or not be) racialized as white. But keeping this multiplicity firmly in mind, referring to whiteness in the singular helps to emphasize that as a social structure and identity marker, whiteness descends from the history of racial capitalist imperialism begun in the late fifteenth century and Euro-US American hegemony, achieved in international politics and economics by the end of the eighteenth century. This history is sketched after the theoretical discussion.

The outline of the historical racial formation and reformation of whiteness is followed by some briefer sketches of specific shifts and redefinitions of whiteness. The sketches focus on how whiteness has been constructed in relation to other groups, encountered by people who thought they were white while those hegemonies were forming or once they were in place. Finally, the chapter ends with a short outline of how whiteness as a term and theory has become a tool to critique and oppose hegemonic racial formation. Combined, the sections of this chapter are suggestive of how whiteness has moved between invisibility and being the center of attention in white-dominated public spheres, the object of deafening silence or a topic of fervent conversation, and variously an object of remembrance and social forgetting.

Whiteness and Racial Formation

There are many theories about the social construction of race and whiteness with great explanatory value. This book frames whiteness as a product of *racial formation*, which sociologists Michael Omi and Howard Winant describe as a sociohistorical process in which racial classifications and identities are created, lived out, transformed, and destroyed via social, economic, and political forces.[1] Racial formation theory makes it easy to balance government and representation, law and culture, and so on, against each other, and point at the reciprocal relationship between different domains of human activity in constructing and maintaining whiteness as a master category in the world today. That doesn't mean there aren't other approaches to whiteness, or even that racial formation is the best among the approaches available. There is no single, "correct" way to look critically at whiteness. Different approaches allow different questions to be asked and different answers to be sought. A primary reason for this theoretical choice here is that it is a broad and flexible theory, which allows for and benefits from the supplementation of other theories.

Racial formation has several constituent parts: racialization, racial projects, racism, and racial politics. Racialization denotes the way that human bodies and appearances, and other markers of physical or visual difference, acquire social meaning. The process of selecting and making various human traits meaningful is central to racialization. These processes aren't neutral but instead reflect social structures, cultural meanings and practices, and power relations. When someone racializes someone else, they also racialize themselves; the construction of an Other is always the construction of a racialized self too, even when racial identity is made invisible, as with whiteness.

Racial classification is unstable and shifting, ultimately arbitrary, and yet not meaningless; because people treat it as real, race functions as a *social fact*. It has consequences such as influencing the distribution of rights and privileges as well as resources and opportunities. Race, then, is strategic, doing political, economic, and ideological work. Thus, for example, independent scholar and activist Theodore Allen wrote, "For when an emigrant population from 'multiracial' Europe goes to North America or South Africa and there, by constitutional fiat, incorporates itself as the 'white race,' that is no part of genetic evolution. It is rather a political act: the invention of 'the white race.'"[2]

The groundwork of racial formation is largely done through "racial projects." To Omi and Winant, "race is a 'crossroads' where social structure and cultural representation meet." It is not possible to explain racial inequality as a purely structural phenomenon because this doesn't "account for the origin, patterning, or transformation of racial meanings, representations and social identities." The opposite applies too: framing race strictly as cultural representation, a system of signification, identity, or cultural attribution, makes it harder to see it as linked with social structures or institutions. Race is never just an idea or concept, but always also part of a structure. Race, then, is both a structure and an accumulated set of meanings that reinforce each other as well as have concrete effects in the world. Thus a *racial project is simultaneously an interpretation, representation, or explanation of racial identities and meanings, and an effort to organize and distribute resources (economic, political, cultural) along particular racial lines.*"[3]

These projects can be large or small, occurring everywhere from the macrolevel of policy making to the microlevel of everyday experience and interpersonal interaction, and are carried out by the dominant and marginalized alike, by individuals, groups, or institutions. They happen in relation and response to broader patterns of race in their sociopolitical context, either to reproduce or subvert, extend or challenge them. Examples of macro racial projects include proposed legal bans of certain kinds of head covering across Europe to target Muslims as a racialized group. Instances of micro racial projects include the proclamation that "Black Lives Matter" or its racist rejoinder "All Lives Matter" as expressions of opposite understandings of contemporary US racial formation. Racial projects build on each other, or stand in conflict, to cumulatively and continuously constitute or oppose the reigning racial formation in any given place or time. At the time of writing, the hegemonic racial project on a worldwide scale seems to be so-called color-blind ideology. As discussed in chapter 6, color blindness can support a white supremacist racial formation that resists the racialization of whiteness while simultaneously masking disproportionate resource distribution to people who are considered white in different contexts. This isn't to suggest that color blindness permeates everything or that it's never challenged, only that it is relatively dominant over other approaches to race and makes it more difficult to disseminate some other ideas.[4] But as Omi and Winant note, the hegemony of color blindness is also "extremely contradictory and shallow."[5]

While race and racism are not synonymous, they are deeply connected. A racist racial project *"creates or reproduces structures of domination based on racial significations and identities."*[6] An antiracist project opposes them. A structural understanding of racism is thus crucial to understanding whiteness. Whiteness is propped up by and props up racist projects in fields such as culture, law, and economics more than it is by explicit, violent hate. This ties into the last aspect of racial formation: racial politics. Racial politics are an ongoing struggle between state and civil society to define and redefine the meanings of race, and can take different forms depending on a nation's political system and structure along with the ways in which race are understood in a given context.

From its beginnings, whiteness has served as what Allen described as a means of "social control," originally put in place by economic elites to prevent social unrest and creating the long-lived idea that whatever else separates white people, their "whiteness" is a more important shared characteristic than, for example, class. This has meant that whiteness has often been defined more by what it is not (Black, "savage," ethnic, or oppressed) than by any positive content. Because of this fluidity, and because "white skin" isn't really white, whiteness is frequently a matter of ascription. As film studies professor Richard Dyer puts it, "White people are who white people say are white."[7] Whiteness is thus in never-ending formation, and the boundaries of white racialization are in perpetual motion.

Origins of Whiteness

Philosopher Achille Mbembe writes that whiteness is, "in many ways, a fantasy produced by the European

Whiteness is thus in never-ending formation, and the boundaries of white racialization are in perpetual motion.

imagination, one that the West has worked hard to naturalize and universalize."[8] It is a fantasy long in the making. Categorizing and ascribing meaning to difference is a common human trait. We often need to categorize to get by and make sense of the world around us. Sometimes this classification is harmless, and sometimes not. It does not always amount to racism as defined above; many ancient texts, for instance, spoke of and ascribed difference to peoples, but did not racialize. It is only with the so-called Age of Exploration, when Europeans reached the western hemisphere, or extended their reach and power deeper into Africa or Asia, that the conditions for a racialized social structure were fully in place.

What would become what we can now recognize as racial formation initially took the language of theology for its model. One particularly common model for arranging beings in the world were cosmic hierarchies, sometimes called a *scala naturae* (ladder of nature) or the "Great Chain of Being." These ladders or chains envisioned all creation as connected in a hierarchy from the lowest to the highest forms of being, frequently with God on top after the rise of Christianity. Attested in antiquity, as early as in the philosophy of Aristotle (384–322 BC), they were topics of much debate throughout the Middle Ages and into early modernity. The *scalae* were often ordered on the level of species. They rarely included racial classifications before the 1600s, when racial thinking entered so-called Western (see glossary) consciousness to stay. Early racial *scalae*, like those of economist and statistician William Petty (1676) or anatomist Edward Tyson (1699), didn't garner much attention, but by the time the aptly named physician Charles White offered his white supremacist *Account of the Regular Gradation in Man, and in Different Animals and Vegetables; and from the Former to the Latter* in 1799, racial classification was a welcome tool for those who wanted to motivate the violent conquest of people, land, and resources.[9]

The essentialism of racial thinking took long to develop. Ancient Greeks, Romans, and others displayed varieties of xenophobia, but almost always with an "escape hatch" in conversion or assimilation. Slow movements toward essentialism in prejudices about European Jewry and Black Africans took place over centuries. While anti-Judaism had been part and parcel of Christianity almost from its inception, it wasn't until the twelfth and thirteenth centuries that some began to speak about an insurmountable difference between Jews and Gentiles, and although the association of the color black with evil has long roots, it didn't translate everywhere into anti-Black sentiment. Spanish anti-Judaism started to include ideas about the purity of blood (*limpieza de sangre*) in the fourteenth and fifteenth centuries, framed in terms of whether someone was Christian or not, rather than in terms of white and nonwhite, but it stands as a historical "segue between the religious intolerance of the Middle Ages and the naturalistic racism of the modern era" in its incipient biologization of difference.[10] Similarly, while it was never universally accepted, the so-called curse of Ham gradually connected Black Africans with Noah's son Ham, who was cursed by his father to be a servant.[11] The curse was the basis for centuries of debate about the legitimacy of enslaving Black people; some used it to motivate enslavement, and others to oppose it.[12]

With the advent of settler colonialism around the turn of the sixteenth century, something else had to take the place of religious language, not least because slavery sat awkwardly next to Christian universalist claims about the unlimited possibility of salvation through Jesus. The so-called discovery of lands previously unknown to Europeans was quickly followed by exploitation, appropriation, and domination. Death followed wherever Europeans went, at the barrel of a gun, but also through disease, starvation, and abusive labor practices. While the word itself wouldn't be coined until 1944, European colonialism was a genocidal project: Indigenous American populations came close to extermination after 1492; the Guanches of the Canary Islands were exterminated between 1478 and 1541; and the native Tasmanians were similarly destroyed between 1803 and 1876. Those who survived colonization were often forcibly moved from ancestral lands, such as in the Swedish colonization of Sápmi starting with the introduction there of silver mining in 1635 and culminating in

1919 with forced relocations lasting into the early 1930s.[13] Many peoples were moved again when the lands reserved for them turned out to be valuable to colonizers after all, as happened to Aboriginal Australians until at least the 1950s, the Lakota Sioux after gold was discovered in South Dakota's Black Hills in 1874, or Indigenous populations in the southwestern United States during the series of forced displacements between 1830 and 1850 known as the Trail of Tears.

New rationalizations were needed to motivate nation building and rapid expansion of world trade, and justify the colonial expansion, exploitation, expulsion, and extermination of Indigenous populations necessary for the profitability of these projects. European encounters with people unfamiliar to them led to questions about whether everyone could be considered part of the same "family of man" and soon thereafter, for example, the moral affordances of enslaving some people. The so-called Enlightenment also focused on ideals of freedom, natural rights, and equality—rhetorics difficult to reconcile with oppression and subjugation. Distinctions between Europeans of different nationalities, or "Europeans" as an imagined supranational grouping, and their Others were manufactured, producing hierarchies designed to order and motivate ideas of human superiority and inferiority. Through racialization, physical characteristics became the basis for social positioning, and ideas about those characteristics were tied to supposed mental, social, moral, and intellectual traits, among others. These folk understandings of difference were then used to inform policy, law, and social organization. It is in this mix of social and economic structures along with the significations and representations of differences between groups of human beings, often on the basis of skin color, that the "master category" of race would be created, with Europe and thus whiteness at its center.[14]

One of the most thoroughgoing early embraces of racial thinking took place in England's North American colonies around the turn of the eighteenth century. The use of unfree labor has a long history. Slavery appears in ancient sources like the Bible or Code of Hammurabi (ca. eighteenth century BCE). The monocultural mass plantation of sugar in Europe and tobacco in British America were both based largely on forms of enslavement of what is now considered "white" people through indentured labor or forced labor for rebels who were deported to the colonies.[15] But in the latter case, in large part because of the increased enslavement of Black people along with the growing labor unrest that threatened social stability and elite profits, a shift would take place throughout the 1600s, after which a system of Black racial oppression and a new racial formation of white supremacy would be firmly in place.[16]

Indeed, chattel slavery is central to the story of the invention of the "white race" in what would become the

United States and elsewhere. Although it is easy to imagine chattel slavery as being an effect of racism, it is more accurate to say that racism was an effect of chattel slavery. Whiteness and Blackness were invented to produce a dividing line between Europeans and Africans in British America. Rich and poor whites were said to have more in common with each other than with anybody not sharing their outward appearance, while Indigenous populations were placed in a separate category. This racial formation was accomplished in part through the interplay between representations of Black people as non- or subhuman, and through laws that, for instance, enshrined racial slavery and the status of Black people as property in the founding documents of the United States. Meanwhile, whites of all classes were successively granted privileges—chief among them, prior to the US Civil War, were the presumption of liberty, right to immigration and naturalization, and right to vote.[17] Historian Nell Irvin Painter notes that "the abolition of economic barriers to voting by white men made the United States, in the then common parlance, 'a white man's country,' a polity defined by race and limited to white men."[18]

The construction of a racially structured society was further accomplished through legislative and cultural means as well as racialized violence. At a time when abolitionism was gaining a stronger footing in the United States, the US Supreme Court's *Dred Scott* decision of 1857 held that Black people—whether free or enslaved—had "no rights which the white man was bound to respect" and codified beyond doubt the racist foundations of the US American polity. What had been known to many by experience was now written in stone: "any 'white' man, however degraded, was the social superior of any African-American, however cultured and independent in means."[19] The decision would be nullified with the abolition of slavery, but the sentiment remained. Reconstruction failed miserably, as has been noted by writers from W. E. B. Du Bois to Carol Anderson, and anti-Black racism only increased in the following decades, bringing with it a wave of vociferous and violent white supremacy. Other socioracial hierarchies were constructed elsewhere by other colonial European powers, some of which are discussed in the next section, and have continued to be constructed into our own time. That doesn't mean all white people were treated as equals, in the United States or elsewhere; rhetoric and reality often diverge.

Efforts to maintain white supremacist racial formations were increasingly couched in scientific language throughout the eighteenth century. Through the taxonomic efforts of naturalists like Sweden's Carl von Linné/ Carolus Linnaeus (1707–1778), whose classification of living organisms (1735) included a division of humanity into different "varieties" (European, American Indian, Asian, and African), race was factored into humankind's place(s) in the Great Chain of Being. Writing in the early 1700s, historian Henri de Boulainvilliers (1658–1722) claimed that France's ruling class was descended from the superior Germanic Franks, linking class to nascent racial thinking. In England, too, myths of superior Germanic blood were foundational to the creation of an "Anglo-Saxon" people, whose imagined racial supremacy formed the basis for a new national identity movement. By the Enlightenment, ideas about "race" had become commonplace and many leading European thinkers of the day were well versed in racializing languages. Although many naturalists like Georges-Louis Leclerc de Buffon (1707–1788) saw differences in pigmentation, for example, as environmentally based, they often nonetheless ranked the "races," assuming white Europeans to be superior at all turns (and those "races" living in less propitious environs as "degenerated" in one way or another).

This is not to say that the "science" of race as it emerged in these years was consistent or uniform. In the 1795 third edition of his pamphlet *On the Natural Variety of Mankind*, German anthropologist Johann Friedrich Blumenbach, who introduced the label "Caucasian" to describe white people, "gamely notes the existence of twelve competing schemes of human taxonomy and invites the reader to 'choose which of them he likes best.'"[20] Blumenbach's own schema of five "races" gained widespread acceptance, but racist theorists have never managed to agree on a stable number of supposedly immutable races. By Blumenbach's third edition, skin color played a large role in what was considered the science of race. He included skin color in his taxonomy and ranked white skin the highest, as belonging to the "oldest variety of man," although skin color was ascribed to climate and experience rather than innate qualities, and "Caucasian" whiteness was extended as far as the Ural Mountains and Ganges. There was also an ongoing struggle in the nineteenth century between people who advocated a monogenetic understanding of humankind's origin and those who advocated a polygenetic understanding. Adherents of the former believed that all human races shared the same origin, whether divine or natural, but had since diverged, while the latter instead believed—heretically to some—that different races had different origins.

By the dawn of the nineteenth century, race was being turned into biology and classified as something ostensibly "natural." Supposedly innate differences between whites and "inferior" peoples were increasingly used as a justification for the unequal distribution of rights and resources, even as doctrines of "natural rights" were widely touted. While other thinkers were more influential at the time, ethnologist Arthur de Gobineau's (1816–1882) posthumous influence would be immense. In his 1853–1855 *Essay on the Inequality of the Human Races*, Gobineau claimed among other things that France's population consisted of three races—Nordics, Alpines, and Mediterraneans—that corresponded to the country's class structure. The scientification of race and whiteness continued through uses of naturalist Charles Darwin's theory of evolution (1859), particularly racialized in so-called social Darwinism, which applied ideas of "natural selection" to humans, and argued that racial and class inequalities were rooted in biological differences rather than social inequities. This worldview was used to oppose social policies meant to help the poor, children, or women, among others, further manufacturing and enshrining differences between not only white and nonwhite people but different classes of white people too. Darwinian assertions were also used to legitimize genocide: the "higher" races were naturally bound to overtake the "lower."

Other schools of racial thought appeared as well, some of which are discussed in more depth in chapter 4; craniometry, phrenology, and eugenics are examples of supposedly scientific ways of measuring racial characteristics used to motivate policy and cultural shifts that privileged certain whites, and oppressed or marginalized peoples of color and other whites. These means of racialization allowed for new forms of racial projects, which helped establish racial formations wherein race-based legal and economic organization could form the basis for naturalization and exclusion from citizenship, residential segregation, and forced sterilization, among other things.

Such racialization processes and racial projects would find their most rationalized expressions in what historian George M. Fredrickson calls the twentieth century's three "overtly racist regimes": Nazi Germany (1933–1945), the Jim Crow US South (1870s–1960s), and apartheid South Africa (1948–1994). All three regimes had explicitly racist official ideologies, expressed their ideas of racial difference most harshly in laws forbidding interracial marriage, legally mandated social segregation, excluded designated out-groups from public office or the franchise, and limited out-group access to resources and economic opportunities.[21] While they differed in their specifics, they all promoted racial formations that anchored and upheld white supremacy against groups defined as nonwhite, whether the major differentiation ran primarily along a color line (white to black) or between different phenotypically white groups ("Aryan" to "non-Aryan"/Jewish).

Although opposition had been brewing for decades, particularly in Black critiques of biologistic or "scientific" racism, it was only around the Second World War and after that established racial thinking was thoroughly challenged in white spaces (and then largely with reference to the critiques offered by white critics). Nazi Party leader Adolf Hitler had, to use Fredrickson's phrasing, given racism a "bad name."[22] The idea that race is a determinative biological fact was reconsidered and labeled a social myth by, for instance, the United Nations. Explicit interpersonal racism largely became unacceptable in white public arenas in the postwar period, while structural racism remained (and remains) largely unconsidered and unaddressed in many of the same spaces. Nevertheless, the explicitly racist legal organization that upheld white supremacy remained in place in the Jim Crow South and South Africa. The forced sterilization of non- or less than white "undesirables" (around sixty-three thousand people, starting in 1935) continued in Sweden until 1976 for the "good of the race." The greatest beneficiaries of the move away from biological race theories were in many cases phenotypically white groups that were granted more secure white racialization.

Omi and Winant write that in our day, race is primarily a political phenomenon. To a great extent, it always was. The meaning of race is often rooted in political contestation between state and civil society, and among different groups in relation to the state; nation-states have been engaged in racial definition for centuries, determining who can be a citizen, who can marry whom, who can reproduce, who can live where, and so on. A given state's racial classifications shape people's status, access, rights, and much more. Those racialized as white in different states frequently work, consciously or not, to maintain their privilege against those not so classified, or engage in a delicate dance to give up enough space to allow some into whiteness while keeping others out. This is not surprising.

Whiteness may be a fantasy, but for many who profit from it, it is a fantasy worth believing in. Being counted as white continues to materially and decisively impact on who can live in what ways in much of the contemporary West as well as much of the rest of the world, and if they can even attempt a life there to begin with.

Some Historical Formations of Whiteness

Race is a nebulous idea. The term has never had a fixed, precise meaning. But while whiteness is a fantasy, racialization has real, palpable effects through the erection of racialized structures of power. The number of races proposed by racial theorists and criteria used for racialization have varied wildly. In addition to phenotypically and often geographically based racial designations (such as "African," "European," or "Asian"), racial assignation has also been based on linguistic traits (Theodore Roosevelt, for example, spoke of "the English-speaking races"), national or ethnic origin (such as the "Irish race," "French race," or "Slavic race"), or religion and culture (e.g., the "Jewish race"). As few as three and up to as many as sixty races have been suggested over the years. Race and whiteness have never been primarily about classification, but rather hierarchy. We see this is across the world and over the centuries. This section will look at a few historical racial

Whiteness may be a fantasy, but for many who profit from it, it is a fantasy worth believing in.

projects meant to erect such structures and thus help cement white supremacist racial formations.

The sixteenth- to nineteenth-century colonial Spanish Americas included a *sociedad de castas* (caste society) structure, ordering social standing by skin color and ethnicity. The three primary racial categories were white, Black, and Indigenous. White people were at the top, and the distance from Spanish whiteness affected access and mobility. In part because Spanish women did not emigrate in large enough numbers, however, *mestizaje* or "mixture" quickly became a concern. Caste labels multiplied to describe offspring of "mixed" relationships: *mestizo* could describe children of white and Indigenous parents, mulatto or *pardo* could depict children of Black and white parents, and *zambo* could mean children of Indigenous and Black parents. Casta labels weren't just about skin color but also culture, clothing, and eating habits, for instance. This is seen in casta paintings, mostly from eighteenth-century Mexico. The paintings functioned both taxonomically and narratively. Frequently done as series, the paintings showed families—usually a man, woman, and their child—made up of different constellations of ethnoracial "mixes." Whiteness and blackness were largely separated, but racialization wasn't insurmountable. During part of the eighteenth and nineteenth centuries, free people of mixed African descent could petition (and pay) the Spanish court for *gracias al sacar*, a royal writ granting whiteness. Casta eventually gave way to *raza* (race) and perhaps less strict social control, but whiteness remains salient in Latin American and across the region; who identifies as white differs greatly, however, based on historical, ideological, cultural, and political factors as well as age and education.[23]

If the castas were fluid, racial formation in the British colonies and later the United States was coming into ever-sharper relief. "When the first Africans arrived in Virginia in 1619, there were no 'white' people there," Allen reminds us.[24] By the end of the century, a strict color line had been erected in culture, policy, and law. The "one-drop rule," which holds that a person with any Black ancestry should be categorized as Black, started as an informal way of upholding the color line in Britain's North American colonies and the antebellum United States, but was codified into southern laws after the abolition of slavery. Similarly, a person's "blood quantum" is a measure of their Native American ancestry. It has been used as a measure in colonial, state, and federal law since the early 1700s to create and assign racial identity to Indigenous populations, thereby limiting citizenship along racial lines. Some tribes in the United States—and Canada—maintain blood quantum requirements as a means of collective survival as well as to secure certain protections from and against the state. One-drop rules and blood quantum have often served to secure white supremacy, as did laws limiting naturalization to "free white persons," such as the Nationality Act of 1790. Citizenship rights were extended to all white men by the 1830s, but racialized limitations continued through, for example, the Chinese Exclusion Act of 1882 or restrictive immigration laws of the 1920s. The United States' status as a white man's democracy was challenged several times, by people still enslaved and Black freedmen, in court cases like *Takao Ozawa v. United States* (1922) and *United States v. Bhagat Singh Thind* (1923), and in other ways. Racial barriers to naturalization remained on the books until 1952, but to this day, secure whiteness remains the lone path to unquestioned citizenship.

The period between 1901 and 1975 saw the rise and fall of what is commonly known as the "White Australia policy," a term that encompasses an immigration doctrine designed to protect white labor from competition from Asian, primarily Chinese, and Pacific Islander labor, and maintain a white majority on the island continent. White Australia restricted immigration except from Europe, and excluded foreign nationals from certain privileges and benefits of citizenship. The policy was among the first legislation passed in the newly self-governing Australia. White Australia figuratively erased, and attempted to literally erase, Aboriginal and Torres Strait Islander populations; Brits had long been considered Indigenous, and the land *terra nullius* even longer.[25] It encoded a racist understanding of white, European Australians as pioneers of civilization surrounded by potential adversaries, helped cement a type of nationalism in the newly formed federation, and served to motivate abuses and the forced assimilation of Aboriginal and Torres Strait Island populations, including policy-driven attempts to "breed out the color" of the national picture. The White Australia policy had a significant impact on demographics and held fast until after World War II, when the desired British migration could not provide enough new white Australians. The restrictions were eased over the following decades. A new Labor government removed the last racial restrictions in 1972 and passed antidiscrimination legislation in 1975 that signaled the end of White Australia in an official capacity. Unofficially, however, the white supremacy that guided the policy remains alive in present-day Islamophobic rhetoric, opposition to Aboriginal and Torres Strait Islander rights, and rejections of multiculturalism.

For all of their differences in scope, scale, longevity, and impact, the examples cited above embody racial projects enshrining supposed racial difference through the aid of legislation, representation, science, or other means. They formed or upheld a racial formation where whiteness was structurally privileged. As noted in the historical overview above, whiteness is not only nor perhaps always even primarily about skin color. White racialization is also about culture, values, social roles, and more, and although the so-called color line is an important metaphor for understanding the organization of societies like the United States, it is important to recognize that it is a metaphor; whatever the rhetoric of white similarity may suggest, not everyone on either side is considered equal to everyone else on the same side. Whiteness has always also been a structure organized along a hierarchy of different forms of whiteness.

Painter, for example, speaks of four "enlargements" of US American whiteness. The first enlargement took place around the turn of the eighteenth century, when the franchise was extended to all free white men and soon thereafter to all (mostly British) white men. The second enlargement allowed German and Irish US Americans into the orbit of whiteness. It rested in part on German and Irish immigrants' service in the Civil War. It also owed to the engagement in race talk by some not-quite-white groups, which embraced racist language to differentiate themselves from Black people. Also important was the arrival of Jewish, Slavic, Polish, Italian, and other eastern and southern European "new immigrants," who were considered less white than Germans and the Irish. The third enlargement followed the Great Depression and World War II, where shared hardships and triumphs, and the fight against a racial dictatorship more explicit than that of the United States, had helped whiten "new immigrants," who gained increased access to the cultural center along with New Deal and Veterans Affairs policies meant to lift

Whiteness has always been a structure organized along a hierarchy of different forms of whiteness.

all boats (except those carrying Black US Americans and others deemed not white). And Painter's fourth enlargement has followed a shift away from making distinctions between different white groups to a more clearly demarcated Black/white color line, across which certain people of color—some Asian, Latinx, "multiracial," and middle-class Black US Americans, for instance—could pass more easily.

Others have offered different understandings of the period discussed under Painter's fourth enlargement. Rather than an "enlargement," legal scholar Michelle Alexander views what Painter describes as a "racial bribe," and historian Matthew Frye Jacobson argues instead for a shift in the post–civil rights era to what he calls "Ellis Island Whiteness"—a whiteness that emphasized a mythical self-image of the United States as a "nation of immigrants" that still ignores nonwhites.[26] While they can take different forms, most enlargements of whiteness work in the service of social control: some groups are granted white racialization that weren't before so that the lines between white and nonwhite can be better maintained and successful challenges be made less likely.

Swedish whiteness also has a history of change. Ever since the beginning of racial taxonomy, Swedes have had trouble classifying the Indigenous Sámi people. Perpetually viewed as non- or not-quite-white, the Sámi continue to be subjected to oppression, forced relocation, and physical and cultural violence.[27] Other marginalized groups have been better able to relocate from the margins of Swedish whiteness to the center. For much of the early twentieth century, Sweden was a leading country in scientific racism, but changed direction in the later half to outwardly became a vocal antiracist and anticolonial ally. By the 1970s, Sweden self-represented as a generous, tolerant, and color-blind country, although more on the international arena than domestically. (As a case in point, as of mid-2021, Sweden has yet to ratify ILO Convention 169, a major international convention on Indigenous peoples, because doing so could put the state in an awkward position in terms of landownership questions with regard to the Sámi.)

While non-Western immigration has increased since the 1970s, whiteness retains a central position in defining who is considered Swedish or not. A main distinction today runs between "Swede" and "immigrant," with the former category framed around whiteness and the latter characterized by nonwhiteness and non-Westernness. Many who were born in Sweden and hold Swedish citizenship but can't pass as white continue to be viewed as immigrants, even into the second or third generation. Adversarial racialization is seen most clearly in widespread anti-Black racism (*afrofobi*) and Islamophobia. Migrants are seen by many as a danger to Sweden's culture, heritage, and welfare state, on which they are figured as a drain.

Meanwhile, as Sweden's demography changes and becomes increasingly nonwhite, Finns and people from the Baltics are being racialized as less ambiguously white, and Greeks, Poles, former Yugoslavians, and others are poised to be let in from the cold of nonwhiteness. Simultaneously, a stricter discursive color line similar to the US model has been erected, affecting who is deemed white against the figure of Black, Romani, Asian, and Middle Eastern–North African Swedes.[28] As before, the boundaries of whiteness shift and warp to keep the center intact, and keep white people comfortable in our privileged existence.

Some Attempts to Understand Whiteness

Many white-racialized Swedes today respond to discussions about whiteness by denying white privilege or making counterclaims about reverse racism. So do many in the United States or Australia, for example. Indeed, the idea that whiteness holds power is foreign to many white people. As noted earlier, white people frequently do not have a racialized sense of self and rarely have to consider themselves in racialized terms. This is one of the ways whiteness manages to hold so much power. But while ideas like white privilege often come as a surprise to many white people who encounter the idea and try to contend with our unearned advantages, it is usually well-known to those who don't have it. While it's impossible to generalize, the existence of a long tradition of people of color discussing whiteness suggests that white people are pretty much alone in not recognizing the power of our whiteness.

What follows is a brief and partial overview of how whiteness has been made visible over the last two centuries. The work of scholars like Robert Fikes Jr., David Roediger, and Veronica T. Watson has been particularly useful in providing wider access to "white life" writing by Black US Americans that date at least as far back as the 1840s. From this written record, spanning many genres and forms,

> whiteness emerges as a way of seeing and knowing
> the world that masquerades as universality and
> remains largely unnamed and unrecognized. It
> is exposed as a mode of social organization that
> is shaped by skin-color privilege and that is
> inextricably enmeshed with other vectors of identity
> such as gender, class, sexual orientation, and the
> organization of space.

This "literature of white estrangement" (or "white exposure") critically engages with whiteness as a social construction, and "present[s] Whiteness as a positionality, or perspective, that refuses to acknowledge its own narrowness, its alarmingly consistent history of oppression, its contradictions and failures."[29] Another notable and relevant form of writing, which had its heyday during the Harlem Renaissance (ca. 1919–1934), was the transgressive "passing novel." In these books and related writings, Black writers portrayed light-skinned or mixed-race Black characters "passing" as white and moving in white spaces. Among the things passing novels accomplished, then, was to highlight the artificiality, absurdity, and fragility of racial thinking, while also playing on white anxieties about racial mixing.

Whiteness studies as it exists today would not be what it is without the critical thought and writing of Black US American writers, activists, and scholars like Frederick Douglass (1818–1895), Anne Julia Cooper (1858–1964), Ida B. Wells (1862–1931), Zora Neale Hurston (1891–1960), Richard Wright (1908–1960), Langston Hughes (1902–1967), Du Bois (1868–1968), James Baldwin (1924–1987), Kwame Ture (1941–1998), Maya Angelou (1928–2014), Toni Morrison (1931–2019), and bell hooks (1952–2021). This is not to say that this literature is a uniquely US American thing, as attested in a particularly strong way by the prominence in whiteness studies of, for instance, Black Caribbean writers such as Frantz Fanon (1925–1961), Stuart Hall (1932–2014), and Sylvia Wynter (1928–). But the critical academic study of whiteness emerged primarily in a US context.

Nor is it to say that literatures of white estrangement are a thing of the past. Literature that includes deconstructions of whiteness as either a primary focus or part of a larger theme can be found in both formerly colonized and formerly colonizing nations. Examples of the former can be found in works by, among others, Nigerian author and critic Chinua Achebe (1930–2013), Kenyan author and literary critic Ngũgĩ wa Thiong'o (1938–), Ghanian author and critic Ama Ata Aidoo (1942–), Jordanian British author and critic Fadia Faqir (1965–), and perhaps unsurprisingly in a large body of literature examining whiteness or critiques thereof in South Africa.[30] Illustrations of the latter can be found, among other places, in officially color-blind and self-professedly antiracist Sweden in works by rapper and author Jason "Timbuktu" Diakité (1975–), author, activist, and entrepreneur Lovette Jallow (1984–), and author and entrepreneur Siduri Poli (1988–), and is a recurring theme in "nonwhite" literature that depicts or deconstructs Swedishness.[31]

This literature and its critical engagement with whiteness extends far beyond what is traditionally understood as "literature." For instance, it is part of the stand-up comedy of South African comedian Trevor Noah and Indian American comedian Hasan Minhaj, comics like Kwanza Osajyefo, Tim Smith 3, and Jamal Igle's *Black* (2016–) or Ben Passmore's *Your Black Friend* (2016/2018), movies like Jordan Peele's *Get Out* (2017), Boots Riley's *Sorry to Bother You* (2018), and Amanda Kernell's *Sameblod* (Sámi blood, 2016), and is ever present on social media. Although admittedly limited, this selection of critical observations of whiteness should be suggestive of the historical and continuing need, wherever white racial formation defines people of color as Other, for many people of color to try to understand as well as maneuver around the power and normative primacy of whiteness.

Alongside this literature, recent decades have seen the emergence of critical whiteness studies as a research area—a sustained, sprawling, and growing academic effort to understand and critique whiteness. Building on the work of mainly Black US American and Black Caribbean writers, such as those mentioned above, and the emergence of emancipatory social sciences around the upheavals of 1968, academic whiteness studies began to coalesce in the 1980s and 1990s. While studies of racism and race as a social construct had a long history by this time, whiteness studies shifted focus to look at how supposedly normal or unraced whiteness is also a racialized category. It needs to be emphasized that whiteness studies is not a clearly delineated field of its own but rather an area of research that stretches across numerous fields and disciplines, united by a common focal point more than anything else.

From its beginnings, critical whiteness studies has cut a wide arc on topics of interest. The main unifying factor initially was perhaps the drive to make whiteness and white supremacy visible, and thus more open to challenge.

Morrison's *Playing in the Dark* (1992) investigated whiteness in the "literary imagination," while Roediger's *Wages of Whiteness* (1991) centered on whiteness and labor history, and Cheryl Harris explored whiteness as property in a legal framework (1993). Peggy McIntosh brought "white privilege" to the fore in a 1988 working paper, and Ruth Frankenberg examined the ways learned and naturalized whiteness impacted white women's lives in *White Women, Race Matters* (1995). Allen studied the political and economic origins of US American whiteness in his two-volume *The Invention of the White Race* (1994 and 1997), while Noel Ignatiev explicated *How the Irish Became White* (1995), Karen Brodkin explained *How Jews Became White Folks* (1998), and Matthew Frye Jacobson's *Whiteness of a Different Color* (1998) offered a more wide-ranging history of how whiteness has been constructed differently at different points in US history. In these and many other books and articles, whiteness studies has concentrated on everything from economics and law to cultural production to the construction and transformation of identities among majorities, minorities, and the ethnoracially in-between. Whiteness studies has continued to expand, developing to encompass more subjects and broadening its horizons, and scholars have come increasingly to view whiteness as a power structure. While whiteness has initially appeared monolithic, scholarship continues to become more sensitive to the local and contextual complexities as well as relational intersectionalities of whiteness. More attention has also been paid in recent decades to pedagogy in studies that look at how whiteness is reproduced in schools, or how schooling can be used to attenuate or challenge white supremacy in various ways.

Geographies and histories of whiteness have multiplied too. Studies of whiteness in or in relation to the United Kingdom and its former dominions—Canada and Australia in particular—have become more common. Whiteness studies has been established in South Africa for at least a couple of decades, and has produced a wide-ranging and in-depth body of scholarship. In other national or regional contexts, whiteness studies has been slower to take hold, but research is emerging in Germany, France, and the Nordic countries. Scholars in each Nordic national context as well as through transnational collaboration have started to look at many of the areas that have been subjected to study in the United States and elsewhere, such as history, law, popular culture, and identity. This overview is necessarily limited by both the space constraints of this book series and language barriers. There is undoubtedly more work out there that is not available to Anglophone readers. But from the above it should be clear that research from outside the United States has continued, expanding the work of early US American whiteness studies by making whiteness and white supremacy more visible, and thus more possible to challenge. And in both the United States and international whiteness studies, critiquing power relationships and structures has also become central.

There is no single "canon" of whiteness studies, nor will there probably ever be. As a research area, whiteness studies is perhaps too sprawling and inter- or multidisciplinary for there to be any one set of standard texts. This is in part why it was relatively easy to name foundational texts above, but more difficult to offer specific examples of influential texts from more recent years of whiteness studies. As an object of study, whiteness is probably too fluid and contextually contingent for an all-purpose collection of "central" works to form. There are no doubt "classics," but even among these works, some are more interesting to sociologists than to historians, or to scholars of culture than of law. This is both a strength and weakness: on the one hand, the risk of unnecessary theoretical reduplication—reinventing the proverbial wheel—or terminological inflation is probably higher, and productive dialogue between scholars and their results may be more difficult; on the other hand, critical perspectives on whiteness can continue to integrate into new fields and disciplines, and provide tools for analysis of even more aspects of the world and people's movements in it.

Whiteness studies has also been criticized for several recurring failings. Early studies in particular are sometimes charged with insufficient sensitivity to context and history. Sometimes a given formation of whiteness appears as if it were formed independent of context or without historical roots. Another common critique is that whiteness studies as a whole has not been focused enough on class and gender, or been intersectional enough. This critique ties closely into other common characterizations of whiteness studies scholars as essentializing or reifying whiteness, presenting it as if it were a single thing, and even suggesting that there is a sort of unified "white gaze" shared by people racialized as white. Too little care has indeed sometimes been taken to consider how people seen as white differ from each other. Conversely, some whiteness scholarship is said to smooth over, ignore, or obscure differences between and among people and groups racialized as something other than white. Combined, whiteness studies can sometimes understandably be seen as erecting a strict white/Other binary, with those situated on either side viewed as monoliths rather than granted the complexity that exists in the real world. Furthermore, whiteness studies has been faulted for re-centering white people's lives too much rather than trying to understand and make visible the impact of whiteness on people of color or those not racialized as white. One final and important critique is that whiteness studies is often seen as being more focused on changing white hearts and minds than on changing policies and structures.

These kinds of critique are important. To be productive, whiteness studies must strive to be historically and contextually sensitive. Whiteness isn't static, nor a neutral descriptor for some naturally occurring phenomenon, but a name given to protean and multiple socially constructed structures of power. In addition to not being static, whiteness is not singular; it alone cannot explain everything, and should be understood as enmeshed with other social formations, like class and gender, to provide convincing analysis and explanation. Neither whiteness nor its relationally constructed Others are ever possible to encapsulate in their complexity. Rhetoric may often discursively attempt to eradicate differences between people racialized as white, but rhetoric is not reality. The constructedness of whiteness in society and scholarship must always be kept in mind. And whiteness studies should never be undertaken to center, indulge, or soothe white feelings.

These issues are in need of remedy, but they are not unique to whiteness studies. Religious studies, for example—a field with a far longer history—continues to suffer from similar failings. While whiteness studies will continue to be redefined, and the growing body of work will continue to fill in gaps and correct errors, there will never be a comprehensive and universally agreed-on definition of whiteness, a history without missed opportunities, or a study that cannot somehow be improved. What some of us call whiteness isn't a thing but instead a construct of language and theory. The word "whiteness" doesn't simply capture something out there, independent of the ways scholars think about, perceive, and experience the world. For these and many other reasons besides, whiteness studies is limited in what it can say and do. Theories and definitions of whiteness in concrete ways construct whiteness as it is understood in any given research context. Scholars should not lose sight of this, but whiteness studies should nevertheless strive to assist in the struggle against white supremacy.

The rest of *Whiteness* will present a series of interconnected overviews of some salient instances of the structures of whiteness, as defined in this book, at play in large and small ways around us. The next chapter presents and discusses six "white words"—words commonly used in public discourse about whiteness. Following this, in order to make the language of whiteness more concrete, chapter 4 examines some important areas in which whiteness intersects with other major categories of social formation, focusing on racial science, class, and gender. Chapter 5 explores one important arena where ideas about whiteness are reproduced and disseminated or contested: popular culture. Using the examples of white children's literature, white superheroes, and white sitcoms, the chapter revolves around how our entertainments, frequently viewed as innocuous and unpolitical, help to disseminate racial formations of whiteness into the wider culture. Having looked at how popular entertainments can uphold and support formations of whiteness, chapter 6 turns to two common contemporary strategies used to keep whiteness out of view and in power: color-blind ideology and discourses about reverse racism. The chapter illustrates that far from being in the service of justice and equity, color blindness is often easily mobilized in defense of white supremacy. The book ends with a brief discussion of different estimations of what the future of what some of us call whiteness should hold and where white racial formation might be heading.

WHITE WORDS

The international public vocabulary about whiteness seems to have grown exponentially in recent years as people try to make sense of an era of resurgent racism in the public sphere and a growing need for antiracist engagement. Another important contributing factor is the accelerated mainstreaming of white supremacy over the past decade or so along with the proliferation of and increased attention—among whites—to police brutality and other forms of state oppression against people of color across the world.

The significance of the internet here cannot be overstated. Whiteness is being talked about by different types of internet denizens for very different reasons in what seems like a set of ever-expanding online discourses. On the one hand, racists, neo-Nazis, self-described white nationalists, and others who seek to defend or celebrate whiteness have fostered a set of online subcultures as well as meeting spaces where they combine this defense with other forms of online engagement. On the other hand, white antiracists are becoming more adept at reading whiteness, and engaging more with people who have known about and have had to maneuver the workings of whiteness all of their lives. Intersecting with antiracist organizing and its languages, white people across the world are becoming better at seeing or critiquing whiteness as a system of oppression, or at least more willing to try. The news and other information media also increasingly use these languages, whether reporting on racist or antiracist events, and to defend, condemn, or normalize white racial formations. In short, whiteness is more often in the spotlight as an object of white public discourse, albeit still in a limited way.

For this reason, this chapter discusses six common terms of this moment. It offers brief definitions of and longer discussions about where these "white words" come from as well as how they are used, and in most cases, outlines how and why they have been critiqued. Together, these discussions will hopefully provide a fuller picture of what is gained and lost in the newfound discourse on whiteness in the white-dominated public sphere—and even the passion for talking about it among, again, both racists and white antiracists. Along the way, the chapter also seeks to supply a foundation for further critical

The significance of the internet cannot be overstated. Whiteness is being talked about by different types of internet denizens for different reasons in a set of ever-expanding online discourses.

thinking about commonly used words and their uses, even when they happen to be words one agrees with.

White Privilege

Feminist scholar and activist Peggy McIntosh offered an influential formulation of "white privilege" in 1988, framing it as a corollary to the negative impact of racism on racialized people. She portrayed this privilege with a metaphor: an "invisible weightless knapsack of special provisions, assurances, tools, maps, guides, codebooks, visas, clothes, compass, emergency gear, and blank checks" about which white people are meant to remain oblivious.[1] Through its workings, white privilege makes unearned power and advantages seem natural and neutral.

White privilege can be described as the accrued historical benefits afforded to white-racialized people in racist and white supremacist societies. It is institutional and structural, not personal and individual. It is available to those of us who resemble the people who hold the most powerful positions in society and dominate its institutions. White privilege means, all other things being equal, having greater access than people of color to power and resources. It affects who can study where, who is more likely to get a job or promotion, or where one can live or get a loan to pay for a house to begin with. In Sweden, for example, immigrants from the European Union, Norway, and Iceland can vote in local elections without citizenship, while immigrants from other parts of the world must wait three years "because they need time to learn the language and understand Swedish culture."[2] White privilege isn't just a matter of the quality of life but also a question of life and death. "There may be no more consequential White privilege than life itself," writes historian Ibram X. Kendi. "White lives matter to the tune of 3.5 additional years over Black lives in the United States."[3] According to a 2021 CDC report, the disparity between Native Americans and white US Americans was 7.8 years in 2019.[4] In Australia, the difference in life expectancy between Aboriginal and non-Aboriginal "females" born in the years 2015–2017 has been estimated at 7.8 years, and for "males" in the same categories, it is 8.6 years. While a concerted effort has been made to "close the gap" in life expectancy by 2030, the target is not expected to be met at the time of writing.[5]

None of this is by accident. Many national histories are built on racist ideas and decisions made by white elites acting on behalf of what they viewed as white people, and rewarding those who best played by the rules. The United States was founded on slavery and Indigenous genocide, and while the circumstances and some laws have changed, the basic racial structures remain in place and continually shift to maintain whiteness. Similarly, although the eugenicist and racist foundations on which the Swedish welfare state were built have been officially dismantled, they linger in structures and cultural memory. And while Britain, France, and other colonial empires no longer serve as extractive metropoles, the white supremacy they fostered hasn't disappeared.

One of the main benefits of white privilege is a firm sense of individualism, while many people of color or nonwhite-passing Others are often regarded in white-centered contexts as group members first. Compare, for example, the common treatment of white mass shooters with that of people of color who commit acts of violence. The former are generally psychologized as individuals, while the latter are almost immediately discussed in group terms, and frequently associated with Islam and labeled "terrorist," even though the "radicalization" of white supremacists and Muslim-identifying radicals is usually similar.[6] Even when white men act in explicit "preservation" of their "race," their individuality is foregrounded.

Because whiteness is "invisible," the idea of white privilege is often surprising to white-racialized people. White people generally don't have a racialized sense of self and frequently consider our advantages earned. Thus while white privilege is increasingly discussed in the public sphere, the counterarguments tend to rest on an individualist or historical basis. The assertions typically hinge on the claim that not all white people are comfortably sitting at the top of the social hierarchy and many ethnic groups were once considered less than white. How, then, can white privilege be real? This is a straw man argument; white privilege discourse has never implied the absence of all hardship. As sociologist Steve Garner puts it, "In these mechanisms, all white people, regardless of class and gender, are ostensibly granted an a priori advantage over everyone else, even if it consists primarily in *not* encountering as many obstacles."[7] White workers don't have the same privileges as the white middle or upper classes. LGBTQIA2S+ whites don't have the same privileges as straight white people. But whatever other privileges white-racialized people don't have, all share white skin privilege, whether we want it or not. Or as philosopher Charles W. Mills notes in articulating the "racial contract" discussed below, "All whites are *beneficiaries* of the Contract, though some whites are not *signatories* to it."[8]

For McIntosh, acknowledging white privilege "makes one newly accountable."[9] An acknowledgment and description of white privilege must be followed by a decision to do something to lessen it. Many have repeated this since: acknowledging white privilege is a first step; the second step is to work to counter it. Something may have been lost in translation, however. For some, considering white privilege in relation to others might highlight personal or structural inequality, while directing the gaze at the self might instead trigger defensiveness.[10] One common critique of the white privilege perspective is that while many are good at the first step, the second one seems more difficult. The need to check white privilege has become a common refrain, but according to critics like Fredrik de-Boer, it risks becoming an end in itself. Often, he claims, acknowledging white privilege fosters self-congratulation and the condemnations of those who have not done so, rather than the work of opposing racism. DeBoer's indictment is harsh: "Anti-racism as mental hygiene is a road that has no ending. The question is whether our goal is to *be* good or to *do* good."[11]

White Guilt

DeBoer's critique of performative white privilege checking is reminiscent of critiques of another white word: white guilt. The idea dates to at least the mid-1960s, when James Baldwin wrote that white US Americans could not avoid seeing "an appallingly bloody history, known all over the world . . . a disastrous, continuing, present, condition which menaces them and for which they bear an inescapable responsibility. . . . The guilt remains, more deeply rooted, more securely lodged, than the oldest of old trees."[12] What the term "white guilt" entails differs between users, but it typically refers to a sense of guilt felt by or attributed to some white people over the harm inflicted on nonwhite Others by white majorities. It's often connected to white privilege, an acknowledgment of personal racist attitudes or behaviors, or feelings of responsibility for the racist attitudes or behaviors of others. The framing can be individual, focused on one's own relation to racism, or collective, revolving around the costs of whiteness as a structure. White guilt can sometimes be a predictor of antiracist attitudes, like support for compensatory affirmative action programs, but at the same time it demonstrates limited political utility.[13] This point unites critics from across the political spectrum.

White guilt is used in several national contexts, but the object of guilt along with the way it is expressed or supposedly expressed differ for historical reasons. In the United States, white guilt is most often associated with slavery, Indigenous genocide, and their continuing effects. In South Africa, it is associated with apartheid, while in France, Australia, or Canada, it is more commonly linked to imperialism and settler colonialism. In the Nordic countries, white (or "Nordic") guilt might be less tied to a colonial past that many are unfamiliar with than to a sense of inequity, and that Nordic prosperity and privilege have been bought at the expense of people of color elsewhere in the world.

However it's framed, the notion of white guilt has its discontents. *National Review* writer Kyle Smith posits a "white-guilt cult" that in his view, perpetuates the racism it disclaims.[14] In an article about South Africa's postapartheid Truth and Reconciliation Committee (TRC), white South African correspondent John Battersby emphasizes collective white privilege and guilt for what had been done in support of white supremacy, but quotes a colleague who rejects the idea that anything was done "in her name": "I do not feel guilty because I'm white. White guilt is a useless emotion. All it does is soothe the rich liberal or confused intellectual's conscience." Thus she rejected a share in apartheid's crimes, even when she had benefited from them.[15] In the Nordic countries, a common response is that the current and previous generations have helped build the welfare society, not passively received it, and therefore there is no reason for guilt over international inequities, or Nordic imperialism and colonialism abroad or in relation to the Sámi.

As with white privilege, then, the usefulness of white guilt is in question. Critics on the Right and Left alike emphasize that it probably does little good. For conservative critic Shelby Steele, guilt "generates as much self-preoccupation as concern for others. The nature of this preoccupation is always the redemption of innocence, the reestablishment of good feeling about oneself."[16] For feminist writer Audre Lorde, it "is only another way of avoiding informed action, of buying time out of the pressing need to make clear choices, out of the approaching storm that can feed the earth as well as bend the trees."[17] Guilt can thus impede deeper reflection or political action.

Battersby wrote that the TRC achieved little, observing that "most of the confessions to it have been tendered—in exchange for amnesty—so cynically, sometimes so arrogantly, they have left the victims not merely unmoved, but even angrier than before." What he sought was "a collective apology from the white community" as well as for white South Africans to acknowledge their white privilege so "you can heal yourself and start to deal with your fellow South Africans on a basis of equality."[18] The critique was structural, but the solution focused on individual emotion just like the TRC itself, which centered national unity and reconciliation at the expense of economic, social, or psychological reparations for apartheid.[19] In 2019 the World Bank determined that South Africa is the world's most unequal country and in 2021, according to the World Inequality Lab, "Asset allocations before 1993 still continue to shape wealth inequality."[20] While apartheid may have been abolished de jure, de facto its legacy remains strong. Calls for a US American TRC are increasing, but it's unclear what it would do. Apologies are clearly not enough; resolutions apologizing for lynching, slavery, and segregation have already been passed (at least three times, in 2005, 2007, and 2009). Everything that led to the protests during summer 2020 still happened; the United States is no less unequal than it was before those resolutions.

That said, some of the strongest critics of white guilt allow for some productive potential. Lorde also wrote that "if it leads to change then it can be useful, since then it is no longer guilt but the beginning of knowledge."[21] Some research suggests that white guilt can lead to the acknowledgment of white privilege, which in turn *can* lead to antiracist action. But it can lead to defensiveness too. This is a common reaction among white people unaccustomed to being racialized as white.

White Fragility

Few contemporary books about whiteness have been discussed as much in white spaces in recent years as sociologist and antibias consultant Robin DiAngelo's *White Fragility: Why It's So Hard for White People to Talk about Racism* (2018). "White fragility" has become a much-used part of the global public lexicon on racism. DiAngelo is credited with coining the term in 2011. The book, which is largely based on her experiences as a corporate antibias consultant, looks at how white fragility is ultimately a way to keep white supremacy in place. The basic argument is that white people are beneficiaries of racial inequalities but unused to thinking about themselves in racial terms, and hence are insulated from racial stress, and feel entitled to and deserving of our advantages (signifying internalized white privilege). The resultant lack of "racial stamina" fosters a fragility in respect to race. As DiAngelo argues, "The smallest amount of racial stress is intolerable—the mere suggestion that being white has meaning often triggers a range of defensive responses. These include emotions such as anger, fear, and guilt and behaviors such as argumentation, silence, and withdrawal from the stress-inducing situation." The evasions and protestations constituting white fragility are ways to not only deflect criticism but also avoid talking about whiteness. They "work to reinstate white equilibrium as they repel the challenge, return our racial comfort, and maintain our dominance within the racial hierarchy."[22]

White fragility of the type outlined above is no doubt prevalent, but how to deal with it has become a matter of debate. Antibias workshops, many critics say, can serve corporations as an alibi. They look good and can help in antidiscrimination lawsuits, but the effects on participants often seem short-term, and companies and institutions that promote diversity training rarely take further steps. Many institutions remain largely white in their upper echelons and don't address structural inequities in the organization. Many companies that hire consultants are themselves major contributors to wealth and income inequality. Workshops are not enough then, critics conclude, nor is it likely that educating individuals about racism and working on themselves will lead to meaningful change on its own.

White Fragility's focus on getting white people to face internalized racism is an important contribution. Yet critics have argued that like acknowledging white guilt and checking white privilege, dampening white fragility can easily become an end in itself. Black, Indigenous, and people of color are largely missing from the book; it's not that people of color aren't mentioned, but their portrayal suggests a lack of agency. While the book includes many helpful diagnoses of structural racism, it ultimately centers on individual relationships and repair. Despite speaking of racism as structural, the perspective on white fragility offered centers white feelings. If white people can internalize a list of "assumptions" about structural racism, this might "interrupt racism," which in turn could change interpersonal relationships and ultimately institutions "because we would see to it that they did."[23] But how this large-scale change can result from personal growth is not discussed. Breaking with "white solidarity" doesn't necessarily lead to building other solidarities. Consciousness-raising isn't a guarantor of change, especially if that consciousness has no clear direction. As David Roediger noted on the book's release, "There is no firm sense of the politics that might be productively attached to the attack on white fragility and white supremacy. . . . DiAngelo elaborates little regarding what comes after white fragility."[24]

Whether DiAngelo coined the phrase or not (the claim is disputed), the idea underlying white fragility is not new. Lorde spoke about it. bell hooks has written about it. Author and activist Austin Channing Brown frames the urgency of white fragility in a clearer way than DiAngelo:

> It ignores the personhood of people of color and instead makes the feelings of whiteness the most important thing. It happens in classes and workshops, board meetings and staff meetings, via email and social media, but it takes other forms, too. If Black people are dying in the street, we must consult with white feelings before naming the evils of police brutality. If white family members are being racist, we must take Grandpa's feelings into account before we proclaim our objections to such speech. If an organization's policies are discriminatory and harmful, that can only be corrected if we can ensure white people won't feel bad about the change. White fragility protects whiteness and forces Black people to fend for themselves.[25]

It might be true, as DiAngelo writes, that racism cannot be ended within the current paradigm.[26] But white fragility extends beyond feelings, and introspection cannot change underlying structures. The question, observes journalist J. C. Pan, "is whether you believe that people's attitudes can be transformed through common struggle or you think that psychological transformation needs to happen before that struggle can take place."[27] The answer is not given, and is likely not an either-or, but answering it cannot rest on the goodwill of introspective white people; the idea of white fragility will never be accepted by all white people, whether in the United States or anywhere else, and whiteness-inspired violence will not pause for the debate to resolve.

White Rage and Racial Backlashes

Journalist Jonathan Capehart writes that "if 'White Fragility' pushes white Americans to see their witting and unwitting role in perpetuating white supremacy, then . . . 'White Rage' shows that fragility in action."[28] The term "white rage" was introduced by historian Carol Anderson following the August 9, 2014, killing of Michael Brown and the ensuing revolt.[29] "Again and again," writes Anderson, "across America's ideological spectrum, from FOX News to MSNBC, the issue was framed in terms of black rage, which, it seemed to me, entirely missed the point."[30] Rather, Anderson saw white rage as the main issue in what had happened. The trigger for white rage in US history has been Black advancement, Black people's desire or drive to make places for themselves within white spaces, and demands for full and equal citizenship. White rage is the effort to keep these ambitions down through legislation, policy, and other repressive means, coupled with the rhetorical maintenance of the moral high ground.

Anderson charts the history of white rage from Reconstruction to former president Barack Obama, showing how time and again, white US Americans have worked to counter Black advancement through legislation to hinder social and geographic mobility, or access to education, housing, and the right to vote, among other examples. White rage is a form of white backlash that has continued since Anderson named it. Much of 2020 was marked by white rage and backlash in the United States, including voter suppression attempts, racialized police brutality, and the racialized impact of and response to government interventions and restrictions to stem the pandemic. Donald J. Trump rode white rage into the White House in 2016, and nearly again in 2020. It took mass organization among Black, Latinx, Indigenous, and other marginalized voters to counter a significant growth in white support for Trump. Critical race and whiteness studies researcher Tobias Hübinette has suggested that the same type of organizing may be necessary to keep white rage from taking over Swedish politics in the 2022 elections.[31]

George M. Fredrickson points to white backlash dynamics similar to Anderson's white rage in other times and places as well, writing that the "projects that brought racism to ideological fruition and gave it the independent capacity to shape the societies and polities of the United

States and Germany in the late nineteenth and early twentieth centuries were organized efforts to reverse or limit the emancipation of blacks in the former country and of Jews in the latter."[32] A particularly prominent recent European example of white rage or backlash on this model is Brexit. More than a referendum on the European Union, Brexit was a "challenge to assumptions about Europeanness, whiteness and belonging" that brought to the fore racist and Islamophobic concerns about the European Union's ability to keep "undesirable," nonwhite Others out.[33]

As such, Brexit is related to the recent rise in influence of right-wing populist, anti-immigrant parties with Far Right backgrounds that have sanitized their images. France's National Rally (formerly the National Front) has switched to a more populist, toned-down xenophobia since Marine Le Pen took over the leadership in 2011. Support grew steadily until a disastrous 2017 debate deflated the rise, but many of the party's ideas have become common political currency in France. In Germany, Alternative für Deutschland has found growing support for its often vociferously anti-immigrant platform since its creation in 2013. Alternative für Deutschland's challenge to the Merkel government's 2015 decision to accept 1.3 million refugees and immigrants has significantly helped the party gain popularity. The Sweden Democrats, founded in 1988 by members of various right-wing and racist organizations along with a Swedish veteran of the Nazi SS, started changing their image in 2005, and by 2010 received their first seats in national government. By 2014, they became Sweden's third-largest party, and have since dominated the public discourse on immigration and related issues, with a nationalist and anti-immigrant stance. Similarly, while the Finns' Party was founded as a "workers' party without socialism," it is today better known for its anti-immigrant rhetoric. Despite or more likely because of this rhetoric, it consistently polls as Finland's second-largest party while it barely registered in polls a decade ago.

These parties all offer supporters a softer, more palatable form of white supremacy than the explicitly racist Far Right many of them emerged from, and an ethnic and economic nationalist politics that promises, through, for example, welfare chauvinism, to favor "true" (read white) citizens over nonwhite immigrants who are perceived as unassimilable. Their rhetoric accentuates the one thing that unites the haves and have-nots of the citizenry as traditionally defined: our white skin. They scapegoat the "newcomers" for the ills of increasingly unequal, neoliberal economic and cultural conditions, and promise their true citizens improvement if they propel them to power, but they rarely deliver.[34] The haves know that driving a wedge between white and nonwhite have-nots can make it harder for them to find common cause. White rage, it seems, is in high supply these days, and it serves well as a means for maintaining social control in white supremacist societies.

What unites these forms of white rage, or white back-lash, is that they work to secure white hegemony. Sociologist Zygmunt Bauman described something in 2016 that W. E. B. Du Bois had articulated over a century before: giving power to those who, in the end, will work against one's own interest might be small price to pay for a sense of superiority.[35] The growing support for these parties, or the election and near reelection of Trump, isn't that surprising. As Tressie McMillan Cottom notes, "Those of us who know our whites know one thing above all else: whiteness defends itself" from change and challenge.[36] It does so with seething, methodical rage through law, economics, policy, policing, and politics, but also through stories about how whiteness itself is in danger and needs defending.

White Genocide and the Great Replacement

Considering how fraught discussion about whiteness frequently is, it is not surprising that conspiracy theories about the future of whiteness would arise. Two related conspiracy theories have proven especially powerful of late: white genocide and the Great Replacement. Both are based on the idea that white people as a group are facing an existential threat.

The notion of white genocide was popularized in US American neo-Nazi David Lane's 1995 "White Genocide

Manifesto," but is employed across the globe. The conspiracy theory claims that the future of white people is being threatened by "deliberate design," effected through integration, multiculturalism, "miscegenation" (race mixing), nonwhite immigration, and violence against white people as well as the promotion of homosexuality, abortion, and declining white birth rates. Many groups have been implicated in the supposed conspiracy, but the theory is most commonly anti-Semitic at its core. Lane's manifesto also coined the so-called fourteen words, a white supremacist motto centered on white genocide that entreats whites to "secure the existence" of white people.[37]

The Great Replacement theory was popularized in 2011 by French author Renaud Camus, for whom mass immigration, demographic growth among nonwhite, mainly Muslim groups, and low white birth rates are part of a "reverse-colonizing" plot engineered by political and financial elites. These elites supposedly view people and cultures as entirely replaceable. For instance, one group espousing the replacement theory has claimed that the Swedish government is distorting demographic data because it is "pursuing a systematic re-population policy . . . to compensate for the low birth rate."[38] The replacement theory has migrated far from its country of origin, and proponents have successfully connected it with anti-immigration and Islamophobic as well as anti-LGBTQIA2S+, antiabortion, anti-Semitic, antifeminist, and antiestablishment narratives.

The two theories, increasingly used synonymously, are deeply interlinked and have come to gain a prominent position in international Far Right circles. They are sometimes connected to similar conspiracy theories such as the Kalergi Plan, the idea that Jewish elites are pushing an antiwhite agenda by changing the ethnoracial makeup of Europe and the United States, or the Eurabia theory, which holds that elites are orchestrating Europe's submission to Islamic rule. Whatever the form, these theories often frame an existential threat to whiteness, "white culture," and "civilization" that must be curtailed, whether through "remigration," segregation, or even genocide.

These ideas are by no means new. Former US president Theodore Roosevelt, a lifelong theorist of race, warned around the turn of the twentieth century about "race suicide." In his view, while the "higher races" of old-stock "native Americans" (primarily whites of English origin) were having fewer children, the "lower races" of eastern and southern European immigrants were having more. Roosevelt "dedicated the last decades of his life to exhorting the better classes to reproduce more lustily in order to meet and, he hoped, overcome the demographic competition of their inferiors."[39] Lawyer and zoologist Madison Grant's 1916 *Passing of the Great Race* (and its revised edition in 1921) dramatized the melting pot as a threat: it may have worked in the days of "old" immigrants, but in the time of the "new" it would spell the end of a white United

States.[40] And in 1920, Grant's acolyte Lothrop Stoddard published *The Rising Tide of Color: The Threat against White World Supremacy*. In the years following, Stoddard's book was championed by then US president Warren G. Harding (and lampooned by writers F. Scott Fitzgerald and Ernest Hemingway). Swedish racial scientist Herman Lundborg repeated similar warnings about racial degeneration in his 1934 *Västerlandet i fara* (The West in danger).

As these examples suggest, earlier instances of white genocide and replacement thinking by other names were not marginal, as is increasingly the case in our time. These theories have long flourished on the margins, but are becoming increasingly visible in public spaces. White genocide– or replacement-style rhetoric has been employed publicly by politicians like Hungarian prime minister Viktor Orbán and Trump, organizations like the English Defence League, Alternative für Deutschland, and the France-based Les Identitaires/Generation Identity, and pundits like Canadian Vice Media cofounder Gavin McInnes, Canadian YouTuber Lauren Southern, or writer and US American columnist Ann Coulter, among others. Anti– white genocide campaigns also unite activists internationally. In the final years of the 2010s, for example, white South Africans were joined by white actors from Fox's New York studios to the streets of Sweden and beyond in opposition to an imagined white genocide in the former apartheid state. And echoes of race suicide can be heard in sanitized white genocide and replacement literature. "Europe is committing suicide," reads the first sentence of British journalist Douglas Murray's 2017 book *The Strange Death of Europe*, or "at least its leaders have decided to commit suicide," Murray goes on, employing the familiar conspiratorial trope of elites paving the way for a racially conceived replacement of white Europeans and their culture, although it is unclear what exactly is being lost.[41] To suggest the perceived appeal of the argument, the book was produced not by some marginal publisher but by worldwide publishing house Bloomsbury Continuum.

The steadily broadening and increasingly acceptable threat assessment in these conspiracy theories and their attendant existential racial dread inspires different types of action. From propaganda to protests to memes to legislative action, the global reach of white genocide and replacement thinking is accompanied by a global range of white backlash. The white rage fanned by conspiracy thinking increasingly spurs racialized violence. Mass murderers Anders Behring Breivik (Norway), Dylan Roof (United States), and Brenton Tarrant (New Zealand) all mention or allude to these theories in their respective manifestos—the last of which was titled "The Great Replacement."[42] In early April 2021, the Chicago Project on Security and Threats published findings suggesting that the replacement theory was a "key driver" and the "most consistent factor" across three studies of the movement behind the

January 6 storming of the Capitol in Washington, DC.[43] Mere days later, Fox News' Tucker Carlson made another impassioned and high-profile defense of the replacement theory. Although the means differ between proponents of these conspiracy theories—Carlson wasn't on the scene in DC, but his ideas were—the goal is the same: to counter perceived threats to whiteness and maintain white hegemony.

White Supremacy

These white words all point in a single direction to the heart of racism as it is commonly understood: the understanding of whiteness as a superior category and white people as a superior people. But white supremacy is a many-faced thing. It's easy to call people like Breivik white supremacists because they give voice to a brutal worldview. It is harder for many people to see, for example, former US president Thomas Jefferson as an important figure in the cementation of white supremacy as something that permeates every aspect of US American life. Yet white supremacy is both a sometimes expressly and sometimes invisibly racist ideology as well as racist structure. It is also a social system.

White supremacy is commonly understood as a belief or doctrine that claims the inherent superiority of the white race. White supremacy in this sense was at the center of scientific racism, European settler colonialism, and the American Revolution. It animated chattel slavery and the "white man's burden" to spread civilization to "savage" peoples. It guided the Nazi Party and Ku Klux Klan, and continues to stir neo-Nazi and other movements today. It is promoted globally by political parties on the fringe and in the mainstream in many countries. White supremacist ideology isn't static. It changes when it has to, and adopts language and strategies from the surrounding societies. Rather than self-identifying as white supremacists, however, many adherents today use euphemisms like "alt-right," "identarian," or "white nationalist." The basic impulse remains the same, though: to promote, rationalize, and secure continued white privilege and dominance.

And this goal has been reached, most notably in explicitly white supremacist states or political units. "In its fully developed form," wrote Fredrickson, "white supremacy means 'color bars,' 'racial segregation,' and the restriction of meaningful citizenship rights to a privileged group characterized by its light pigmentation." White supremacy as ideology or doctrine, then, is aspirational. White supremacy as a structure is grounded in "systemic and self-conscious efforts to make race or color a qualification for membership in the civil community."[44] This understanding of white supremacy describes a system of white domination rather than any belief or doctrine. In this sense, white supremacy perhaps applies more than anywhere else to US and South African history, but such racialized social, political, and economic orders have been successfully sought and at least partially operationalized in many nations.

Neither white supremacy as ideology nor as systemic praxis can cause themselves, however, and they cannot stand without a firm foundation. According to Mills, "White supremacy is the unnamed political system that has made the modern world what it is today." White supremacy in this sense is a local and global sociopolitical paradigm that Mills frames as a racial contract "between between those categorized as white *over* the nonwhite" to effect "the differential privileging of the whites as a group with respect to the nonwhites as a group, the exploitation of their bodies, land, and resources, and the denial of equal socioeconomic opportunities to them."[45]

The racial contract is political, moral, and epistemological. Politically it creates a polity, state, and juridical system on a racial basis, and morally it establishes racially differential rules and obligations. In this way, societies that privilege whiteness can be created and maintained, and states that maintain whiteness can be formed. The racial contract also requires its own moral and empirical epistemology, or its own "norms and procedures for determining what counts as moral and factual knowledge of the world." Mills writes about an "epistemology of ignorance" (and later about "white ignorance"), under which what counts as a "correct" and "objective" interpretation of the world in a white polity is based on a (tacit) agreement to misinterpret the world: "One has to learn to see the world wrongly, but with the assurance that this set of mistaken perceptions will be validated by white epistemic authority, whether religious or secular."[46] It is an agreement among whites to see the world as fair and neutral rather than built on white privilege and oppression.

This epistemology of ignorance fosters false perceptions of the world and misunderstandings that allow for the continued production as well as reproduction of white supremacy. It promotes whiteness-favoring understandings of right and wrong, past and present, truth and falsehood. Education, entertainments, news reporting, and other sources of knowledge share in the maintenance of this ignorance, and make it more difficult to see, or easier not to see, Baldwin's "appallingly bloody history" or the many ways whiteness affords privilege in the present, for example. It thus contributes to and upholds the invisibility of whiteness and white supremacy.

Speaking Whiteness

This chapter has barely scratched the surface of the wide range of white words circulating in the current moment. It could have focused instead on "white shame," "white nationalism," "white terror," or "white pride," for instance. Nor has the chapter delved overly deep into the words included. It has been designed to discuss some of the ways that whiteness is being made visible and offer some background for the current public discourse, but also provide ways of thinking about some of the opportunities and limits of this political moment in the history of whiteness.

For much of its history, whiteness has thrived by being invisible to those who benefit from it. This has always been by design. If more people had been more aware of what has been done in our name, and exactly what the cost has been and continues to be for the relative ease with which we move through the world, white supremacy *may* have been a bit harder to maintain. That is not to say that simply naming whiteness will be enough to end its hegemony or that historical injustices would simply not have happened if only there had been a critical theory to get at their roots sooner. That would be naive in the extreme. After all, atrocities have been committed in the name of white supremacy by people who had no illusions about what they were doing or why, and the current historical moment's attention to whiteness has neither ended racism nor dismantled white supremacy.

But the language we use has consequences. It can influence whether we take action and how we do so. Common white words like white fragility, white guilt, and white privilege have been explored here not only in terms

The language we use has consequences. It can influence whether we take action and how we do so.

of what they can do but also how they can become ends in themselves, rather than the springboards for action and engagement they can be. Similarly, words like white genocide can inspire action and engagement in the service of white supremacy. To be sure, the alt-right's lethal foray outside the online world in Charlottesville, Virginia, in 2017, and quick retreat exemplifies how many contemporary white supremacists tend to shy away from large-scale, high-stakes public events. Still, the growth of online white supremacy should not be discounted; its rhetoric continues to find fertile ground and keep the embers of white rage burning white hot. This was made clear again on January 6, 2021, in the chaos of the white supremacist riot at the US Capitol. Along with the growth of white supremacist populism, white supremacists continue to pose one of the greatest threats to national safety and security not only in the United States but in France, the United Kingdom, Germany, and Sweden too. Speaking about, thinking about, and remembering the damage whiteness can do is crucial so long as the structures described by the white words above continue to exist.

IT'S A WHITE WORLD AFTER ALL

Whiteness doesn't just exist. It must be spoken, thought, legislated into existence, or otherwise manufactured. It must be maintained and reproduced. Neither does it affect people equally or afford everyone racialized as white the same privileges. The notion of racial formation has already been discussed, but like most social categories, whiteness doesn't stand alone. It isn't just a matter of race but intersects with, and it is affected by and affects, other master identity categories as well. To better understand how whiteness can take and change shape, it is useful to consider it in light of the idea of intersectionality, first introduced in the field of Black feminism.

The term "intersectionality" was coined in 1989 by Kimberlé W. Crenshaw. At the core of the term and theory of intersectionality is the understanding that people

Whiteness doesn't just exist. It must be spoken, thought, legislated into existence, or otherwise manufactured.

experience discrimination and power dynamics differently, based on different, overlapping identity categories.[1] The way these identities intersect creates different subject positions in relation to reigning social formations. Masculinities and femininities are seldom only gendered; they are, for example, also raced. Even though they are both men, say, a Black man and white man are likely to experience the world differently as well as be viewed, treated, and understood differently—because the ways they are racialized affects how they are perceived as gendered beings too. The same is likely to be the case for a Black woman and white woman; they are both women, but the former is a *Black woman* and the latter a *white woman*, and the adjectives signify a world of difference. Similarly, a straight white man and gay white man are likely to experience different obstacles or privileges because of sexual formation. Both are white men, but in a heteronormative society, queerness is often suspect. How suspect again depends on whose queer identity; violence against Black trans women was highlighted during several Black Lives Matter protests in 2020 in recognition of the vulnerability of an especially marginalized demographic.

Intersectionality is a way to both observe and critique the power structures behind these overlaps and seek their elimination. It is most frequently used to identify and critique intersecting and overlapping identities to identify sites of oppression, but the theory also acknowledges that identity intersection and overlap can promote privilege. As such, it is a useful and necessary tool for the study of whiteness: on the one hand, it can help to dismantle the central idea that whiteness unites those racialized as white in a shared identity; and on the other hand, it can help explain how despite making universalist claims about women's or worker's rights, for instance, white feminism and labor movements have historically often been built on white supremacist foundations, and served to exclude those with whom activists had more in common than they would or could admit.

Whiteness permeates nearly every aspect of life in our world in some way. Discussing every social, cultural, political, economic, or other structure that is affected by and affects whiteness in a single chapter isn't possible. Rather, this chapter looks at versions of three topics that are sometimes described as the "trinity" of social science: race, gender, and class. Since this entire book builds on a racial formation framework, the focus is narrowed to speak to race as a question of science in the past and present. The discussions about gender and class attempt to take a broader perspective, speaking about them in relation to social, economic, and cultural factors. This inevitably means that these surveys are broad, but suggestions for more in-depth reading are provided in the further reading section.

Eugenics and the "Science" of Whiteness

Aside from the need to find proof for the difference between so-called races, one recurring problem for promoters of white supremacy is the existence of people who "look white," but do not fit with the preferred image of whiteness. For as long as there has been a "white" category in the imagination of race theorists, there has been a need to make distinctions and explain away embarrassing exceptions to supposedly hard racial rules. As has been noted, promoters of white supremacy have sought the "purest" form of whiteness, locating it more often than not in the English, Scandinavians, Germans, or their ancestors. Many of the same people have also worked hard to argue for the existence of more than one "European" race to "prove" that only one is truly worthy.

Among the most powerful tools employed historically for this purpose are "scientific racism" and the subfield of "eugenics." They emerged when science was becoming increasingly legitimate and authoritative. In gaining explanatory legitimacy, science also became a means for the powerful to exert control. Scientific racism and eugenics, in their own time widely accepted, provided biopolitical models for sustaining whiteness and white supremacy by creating supposedly objective justifications for inter- and intraracial hierarchizing and inequalities. "Biopolitics" here refers to the politics that governs and holds power over life and populations, supervised through "regulatory controls" of biological processes related to such things as propagation, birth and mortality, and life expectancy and longevity.[2] While biopolitics can work to maximize health outcomes for the common good, it also often works to segregate and hierarchize, to create and uphold domination and hegemony. Around the turn of the twentieth century, for example, Sweden's race-based and social Darwinist *lapp skall vara lapp* (lapp shall be lapp) politics split the Indigenous Sámi population in two: those who herded reindeer and those who didn't. The goal was to assimilate the latter, who would cease to be Sámi at all, while the former, viewed as wholly different, were to be segregated from the majority society. A paternalistic argument in favor of these policies claimed that if the "true" Sámi were to grow accustomed to "civilization," their culture would die out. There was an ample exchange of ideas and data between the administrators of the segregated Sámi school system and Swedish eugenics researchers.

Scientific racism and eugenics have allowed political interests to be couched in the language of science, and thus be made to appear natural rather than rooted in specific ideologies. The ideas of scientific racism were used to support and legitimize the building of Western wealth, power, and hegemony on the backs of supposedly inferior races. Chapter 2 has already charted much of the prehistory of scientific racism. In this perspective, race is a driver of history, an inescapable fact of human life. By the turn of the twentieth century, racial determinism was widely accepted as fact, and the ideas of scientific racism would continue to gain stronger footing through the 1940s. Scientific racism had many offshoots, among them craniometry, which centered on the measurement of human crania to determine racial origins, or the associated phrenology, which used the measurement of skull features to determine or predict personal or mental characteristics.

As the twentieth century dawned, the United States had a fourfold racial hierarchy: northern Europeans were positioned at the top; "new immigrants" below them; Black people were at the bottom; and Indigenous Americans and Asians were barred from citizenship. But embarrassingly, there were poor whites of supposedly superior racial stock who could not readily be accounted for in this scheme. One way out of this bind was found in the notion of "degeneracy." Pseudoscientific ideas that defective blood was creating defective humans, who through heredity were passing along undesirable traits—like sloth and shiftlessness, debauchery and whoredom, pauperism and idiocy—gained popularity. Many influential white people argued that something must be done about it.

This type of thinking was not limited to the United States, nor did it find its most influential initial expression there. Rather, Francis Galton (1822–1911), the English cousin of Charles Darwin primarily remembered as the "father" of statistics, had tied heredity to social prominence as early as 1869 in a book many regard as the urtext of eugenics, *Hereditary Genius: An Inquiry into Its Laws and Consequences*. The term "eugenics," which combines the Greek words for "good" and "inheritance," would soon become a social commonplace. The "science" of eugenics was developed, standing on two main legs: first, there was so-called negative eugenics, the purpose of which was to find ways to keep those deemed inferior from reproducing and passing along their degeneracy, which was supplemented with so-called positive eugenics, designed instead to promote the reproduction of "superior" stocks of people. Both rested on biopolitics; the aim was to develop certain populations through social policy and other disciplining measures, enacted and enforced from the state down.

Eugenics quickly spread from the United Kingdom to most of the Western world, and gained particularly strong footholds in the United States, Germany, and Sweden. But eugenics also found fertile ground in Brazil, China, India, the USSR, and Japan, among other countries. It had no political color; conservatives, liberals, and radicals of all stripes could find something that attracted them in eugenics. While there were no doubt nationalist eugenicists, the "perception of an international of the 'white race' was a driving force in establishing and expanding the international eugenics movement."[3] And this new "science" was by no means marginal: Harvard University was one of its centers in the United States, along with the influential Eugenics Record Office in Cold Springs Harbor, New York; a group of white Swedish elites successfully lobbied for a state-funded "racial biology" institute in 1922, the first of its kind; and in Germany, eugenics was a cornerstone of the Nazi regime. There was frequent exchange and collaboration across national borders; the Nazi regime found much inspiration in US American eugenics research and racial legislation.

Eugenics reached its zenith in the 1920s and 1930s. At its peak, eugenics was applied in several political, educational, and medical institutions and arenas. To differing extents in different countries, it was used to biopolitically regulate the right to citizenship, reproduction, and even life, as seen in the Nazi's euthanasia programs and genocidal campaign. Several states passed laws allowing the forced sterilization of variously defined "undesirables"— often based on mental, psychological, or racially conceived differences—starting in Indiana and Virginia in 1907; Virginia's law was upheld by the US Supreme Court in 1922. There were between fifteen and twenty thousand forced sterilizations in California alone between 1909 and 1923. Similarly in Canada, Indigenous populations were subjected to forced sterilization between 1928 and 1972. Sweden's forced sterilization program began in 1935, focusing first on mental illness and "deficiencies," and later (in the

1940s–1950s) targeting asocial behavior, alcoholism, and vagrancy. Proportionally, Sweden's "traveler" populations were most severely affected. Between 1972 and 2013, five hundred transgender Swedes had to agree to undergo sterilization before being allowed to transition.

Scientific racism provided a major point of intersection and overlap of identity categories as well as motivation for the oppression and marginalization of those people claimed to be inferior. Eugenics more obviously transcended racial categories in its intersectional oppression; it was frequently used to patrol and normalize social formations of gender (free white men were privileged over free white women), and increasingly applied along lines of ethnicity (Jews and other "new immigrants" were deemed unassimilable), mental health or physical ability, and sexuality. As such, scientific racism and eugenics can be viewed as sites where throughout their history, racialization and racial politics, representation and structure, could be linked through racial projects to give racial formation a natural appearance.

In their heyday, scientific racists and eugenicists could use the legitimacy and appearance of objectivity that scientific language holds for many to make such arguments. Today, scientific racism and eugenics are frequently held up as prime examples that the hard sciences are not immune to subjectivity or abuses of power. After World War II, scientific racism and eugenics slowly lost much of their salience. While race has been long discredited as a biological fact, however, it remains very much a social fact. Thus rumors of scientific racism's and eugenics' demise may have been exaggerated. As race, gender, and law scholar Dorothy Roberts has noted, biological race is still an ongoing concern: "We're seeing it in the development of race-specific drugs, in reproduction-assisting technologies, genetic ancestry testing companies that claim to identify customers' racial identities, and DNA forensics used by law enforcement."[4]

Roberts views these phenomena as a new "biopolitics of race" that attributes health and other inequalities to inherent genetic differences, reinforcing inequality and upholding white privilege. The long and continuing history of US medical racism supports this view: structural racism is a fundamental determinant of health disparities and outcomes, and the medical profession is mired in racists structures and stereotypes, from medical school to practice.[5] The American Medical Association affirmed that racism is a threat to public health in November 2020. The impact of structural racism on health disparities and outcomes has also become a topic of public conversation in other countries, such as the United Kingdom and Sweden, in the wake of the COVID-19 pandemic, which has disproportionately affected minoritized people and people of color in many places.

Race is still considered a biological category in some hard sciences and used to classify people, particularly in pharmacogenomics, a field devoted to tailoring medication to people's genetics; it is commonly used in genealogy too, and racial classification has seen a resurgence not least because of DNA self-testing from companies like 23andMe, which reports results based on primarily racially defined "reference populations." It is also seeing a resurgence in marginal yet increasingly normalized pseudoscientific discourses, like those surrounding "race realism" and "evolutionary psychology," which both turn difference back into biology, and thus turn social inequalities between so-called races, genders, classes, sexual orientations, and other social categories into natural inequalities.

Eugenics is today widely discredited as a pseudoscience, but eugenic practices and some of their assumptions remain in public discourse, from the common belief that wealth and intelligence are connected to various forms of popular culture. As an example of eugenics-inflicted popular culture, the liberally slanted comedy movie *Idiocracy* (2006) is premised on the idea that rampant breeding by "lesser" stock (embodied in a "white trash" caricature family) leads to social degeneration. The forced sterilization of Black and Native women continued in the United States into the 1970s and 1980s; California prisons sterilized incarcerated women between 1997 and 2010; and involuntary hysterectomies were reported in Immigration and Customs Enforcement facilities as recently as 2020. Fetal diagnostics, genetic counseling, and other reproductive technologies have clear roots in eugenic thinking even though they are rarely explicitly eugenic in intent.[6]

Eugenic ideas have high-profile academic proponents as well. In a 2009 interview, acclaimed Swedish ethicist and Marxist Torbjörn Tännsjö said about fetal diagnostics that "it's not wrong to want perfect people." Being able to select away not only Down syndrome but also dyslexia, color blindness, and "other weaknesses" would be a net good; it would lead to a better, more equal society. Such negative eugenic practices should be individualized, Tännsjö added, but would lead to a more competitive society. He doesn't claim that "developmentally disabled" people live lower-quality lives, and doesn't want coercive state eugenics, but the argument seems to land in the opinion that Swedish society as a whole would be better off without those "weaknesses" and in favor of a neoliberal eugenics.[7] And in 2020, evolutionary biologist Richard Dawkins defended the scientific soundness of eugenics when he tweeted that it's one thing to "deplore eugenics on ideological, political, moral grounds," but the selective breeding of humans would nevertheless work in practice, like it does with any other animal. "Facts ignore ideology," he wrote.[8] Selective human breeding may be possible, but eugenics has never been only about the science. Eugenics seeks "betterment" or "improvement" in human genetic stock. These are not neutral, descriptive terms. Deciding what is better for a race, *Volk*, *folk*, or other imagined category is inevitably an ideological, political, and moral judgment. After all, what gene determines vagrancy, poverty, or whoredom?

Scientific racism and eugenics have always relied on the equation of science with truth. As theoretical physicist Chanda Prescod-Weinstein notes, "Science's greatest myth is that it doesn't encode bias and is always self-correcting."[9] On the contrary, science has always been complicit in violence and oppression; it was crucial to the invention of race, imperialist globalization, social formations of gender and sexual inequality, and much more. Science as generally understood in the West has always been implicated in the construction of whiteness. But the common narrative of science remains one of enlightenment and progress. As long as this one-sided story continues to be uncritically reproduced, it's likely that science will remain complicit in maintaining oppressive structures of all kinds.

Whiteness and Class

In *White Trash: The 400-Year Untold History of Class in America* (2016), a book that defines neither class nor whiteness, nor how they are made or intersect, historian Nancy Isenberg delivers a paean to poor US American whites' history of suffering. The narrative focuses on "white working-class" concerns to the extent that the struggle for school desegregation in 1950s Little Rock, Arkansas, centers the plight of white racists over the oppression of Black people. In the attempt to bring the supposedly "untold" history of class into US history, Isenberg takes race out of it. The implicit answer to the question "Who were the winners and losers in the great game of colonial conquest" is given already in the title.[10] The book thus exemplifies a common tendency to ignore how whiteness and Blackness were constituted together, how their invention was intimately connected to economics along with the racialization of servitude and labor, and how racialized class structures have very few real winners.

In many colonies, white colonial powers could grant privileges to local elites and use those elites to effect social control over other social strata. That was more difficult in settler colonies like the future United States, where European settler-workers expected to share the wealth. The invention of whiteness was justified by nascent scientific racism, but whiteness is generally understood to have been created from economic concerns. Racial differences were entrenched to motivate colonial exploitation and the enslavement of Black people or people of color, and foster a sense among lighter-skinned lower classes that they had more in common with the white elite than with fellow laborers. As such, it is extremely difficult to separate race from class.

Whiteness as a social control system wasn't constructed overnight, and the white elites' fears of laborers didn't come from nowhere. One example is Bacon's Rebellion in 1676, in which members of "what the planter elite fearfully called a 'giddy multitude'—a discontented class of indentured servants, slaves, and landless freemen, both white and black"—rebelled against wealthy Virginia elites, originally to claim more land from Native populations.[11] To avoid further class rebellion, the planter class offered a "racial bribe" by deliberately and strategically "extend[ing] privileges to poor whites in an effort to drive a wedge between them and black slaves. . . . Poor whites suddenly had a direct, personal stake in the existence of a race-based system of slavery."[12] People racialized as white were allowed freedom of movement and assembly, owning property and weapons, and being educated; people racialized as Black or nonwhite weren't. The fact that "lower-class" whites could patrol the mobility of enslaved people in Britain's North American colonies and the United States puts a fine point on the idea that whiteness is a system of social control. Many poor white settlers may have found their hope of joining the propertied gentry dashed, but at least they had their whiteness.

The idea that whiteness could be a form of property was introduced by critical race theorist Cheryl L. Harris.[13] Whiteness was quickly enshrined in law, and became the defining characteristic of free human beings in contrast to Black enslavement and the defining characteristic of the right to possess land in contrast to Native Americans' supposedly improper forms of ownership. (Similar arguments were made regarding the ways, among others, Aboriginal and Torres Strait Islanders as well as the Sámi interacted with the land they inhabited, and how that gave white settlers or the state the right to take these lands for their own.) With whiteness came the franchise, economic mobility, and what W. E. B. Du Bois called "public and psychological wages": public deference, social access to white and public spaces, a measure of leniency in court or deference from elected officials who depended on their vote, better schools, and so on.[14] Central to the emergence of whiteness as property was the right to exclude. Even though scientific racism carries less water today and de jure segregation has been abolished, the public and psychological wages of whiteness are still being offered in the expectations fostered by white privilege.

Since whiteness supplies significant wages and privileges, American studies scholar George Lipsitz's argument that there exists a "possessive investment in whiteness" should come as no surprise. Whiteness, writes Lipsitz, "has a cash value"; it accounts for advantages related to unequal relations in discriminatory housing markets, education, hiring practices, and opportunities for intergenerational wealth, among other areas. Because of this, white US Americans are encouraged to "invest in whiteness, to remain true to an identity that provides them with resources, power, and opportunity."[15] Although the historical circumstances differ, whiteness functions as property in other places as well, and white people have been and continue to be encouraged to invest in whiteness internationally.

David Roediger, in his Du Bois–inspired *Wages of Whiteness* (1991), has argued that white US American working-class consciousness emerged in the 1800s on a racial foundation; white workers united around whiteness and the presumption of freedom attached to it, primarily against the unfreedom that ideologically defined Black US Americans under white supremacy. Overlapping this history, the white labor movement in Sweden engaged in its own racial projects and politics. Between the 1850s and 1930s, it developed a form of what historian Håkan Blomqvist calls "socialist whiteness." This whiteness was not understood primarily through skin color but instead "as ethnocentric ideas about European civilizational and national superiority wherein race and ethnic particularity were important elements." The white working class was styled as a carrier of Sweden's national and cultural characteristics with reference to the scientific racism of the day, disseminated in part through *folkbildning* (mass education). The white working class emerged as the true heart of the nation, contrasted against exploitative and internationalist capitalists as well as eastern European imported labor—Slavs, Russians, and sometimes Jews. Rather than Roediger's color-rooted wages of whiteness contra Black US Americans, Swedish workers could find a social capital in whiteness: "Swedishness, civilizational belonging, and racial worth could be made into an asset to invoke against powerlessness and in defense of internal and external threats."[16]

Swedish socialist whiteness began to wane with the rise of Nazism, but its ideas were not unique, nor did they disappear. One school of scientific racism held the Nordic race in particularly high regard and counted Swedes as the "purest," and thus most valuable and beautiful, of white folk. This conception was central to Sweden's early 1900s' shift from empire to nation and the Social Democrat–led construction of the so-called Swedish *folkhem* (people's home) welfare state between around 1918–1950.[17] To preserve the race and stop mass emigration to the United States, the franchise was expanded, entitlements and benefits were established, and an ideal of class equality was widely touted. The emphasis was decidedly on the *folk*, the people or race. Eugenic or race-preserving laws were adopted to regulate birth control and abortion, adoption and marriage, and migration. Eugenic propaganda was disseminated in schools and the military. From 1934 until 1975, the forced sterilization of "lesser" people was balanced with incentives for "purer" specimens to reproduce. Sweden's working-class white men went from being considered qualitatively Other from the higher classes to being fully incorporated into the nation, tasked with maintaining and further building its supposed superiority; women were mainly tasked with reproducing the race in the domestic sphere.

Starting gradually in the 1950s, however, Sweden's self-image and international reputation began to shift toward that of an ally of the oppressed and color-blind, antiracist "global conscience." In recent decades, the welfare state's social safety net has been partly dismantled by neoliberal politics. Nevertheless, the *folkhem* image remains strong and cast in an exclusionary vein. While Sweden at the time of this writing has one of the world's few officially antiracist and feminist governments, it is today also one of the so-called Western world's most ethnoracially segregated countries in residential, labor, and educational terms. This inequality is intergenerationally transmitted. Meanwhile, among so-called ethnic Swedes (i.e., Swedes understood as white), unemployment remains low and poverty remains rare. Clearly, whiteness has a robust cash value in Sweden as well.

Political discourse continues to encourage possessive investment in Swedish whiteness. Sweden's three largest political parties at the dawn of the 2020s—the Social Democrats, Moderates, and Sweden Democrats—all style themselves as champions of working- and middle-class interests and the welfare system, and all engage in classed whiteness rhetoric. In 2010, the Sweden Democrats released an election ad in which a group of burqa-clad

Muslim women pushing strollers race a white pensioner to claim the last dregs of the state budget. The ad tells viewers that on election day, they could decide whether to limit immigration or pensions. Pitting immigration against pensions was a ahistorical wedge tactic—Swedish pension funds had been assailed by neoliberal reforms since the mid-1990s—but it was rhetorically powerful: new, foreign elements were taking money out of the hands of the people who had built Sweden. Although the ad was quickly pulled from rotation, the party's anti-immigrant rhetoric was successful, and it gained its first-ever seats in Swedens's *riksdag* (parliament). Mixing anti-immigrant rhetoric with *folkhem* imagery, the party has continued to attract working-class and union member voters, particularly among white men, and consistently polls as a top-three party.

The Sweden Democrats' position has dominated political discourse on immigration, and competing parties have adopted similar language. Increasingly, the leading parties talk about law and order, welfare abuse, and otherwise blame immigrants for the increasingly vulnerable position of the welfare state. An October 2020 social media post by the Social Democrats blaming migrant workers for wage dumping and "plundering our welfare" is a recent example of Sweden's leading parties joining the international lamentation that "foreigners are taking our jobs" (figure 1). In Sweden, as in the United States and elsewhere, this

Socialdemokraterna ✓
@socialdemokrat

Den okontrollerade arbetskraftsinvandringen dumpar svenska löner, plundrar vår välfärd, utnyttjar utländsk arbetskraft & bidrar till finansieringen av organiserad brottslighet. Det är ett befängt system som måste göras om i grunden.

Figure 1 "The uncontrolled labor immigration dumps Swedish wages, plunders our welfare, exploits foreign labor & contributes to the financing of organized crime. It is an absurd system that must be fundamentally redone." Post by Sweden's Social Democratic Party, October 23, 2020.

rhetoric projects structural elements rooted in politics, finance, and corporations at the national center outward to the margins, shifting blame for policy and exploitation onto the marginalized. Here, racism against nonwhites is balanced perfectly with the function of whiteness to smooth out differences among people racialized as white: the political and economic elites—who have done far more for far longer to damage the Swedish welfare state than any "foreigners" have—are considered part of the beleaguered "us" against whom a unified, foreign, nonwhite "them" is discursively arrayed and politically punished. As largely white elites dismantle protections and push people of color to the social and urban margins, the costs of that marginalization is paid twice by the marginalized through both lower overall living standards and racialized over-policing. As Lipsitz puts it, in neoliberal structures, "the people who *have* the most severe problems are seen *as* problems through this lens."[18]

In Sweden, the United States, and many other places, nonwhite people's protests against classed inequalities are often dismissed. In September 2020, employees of SR, Sweden's public service radio, launched a complaint that the institution didn't represent Sweden's population in either its organizational structure or the content of its programming, and that many employees have encountered racism in the workplace. SR's CEO responded that she was "saddened" that the accusations were made and denied there was a problem.[19] By February 2021, the repercussions were clear: employees of color reported how they had been disbelieved and dismissed, and reporters of color had been expressly forbidden to report on Black Lives Matter, racism, or racial representation, and implicitly discouraged from reporting on racism at all.[20] Swedish media is largely white; so are the corporate and nongovernmental organization fields, for example. The country's internationally unique for-profit private school system is a major driver of segregation. Despite these and other findings about structural inequalities, it is still common to see denials that racism exists in Sweden and the blame shifted to nonwhite people themselves, such as that they live "outside" regular society, "it's their culture" that leads to their failures, "they refuse to integrate," and so on. A 2021 study shows that 49.3 percent of Sweden's population is working class, but the majority nevertheless continues to identify as middle class.[21] The working class is symbolically annihilated in media and discourse, and the lowest rung, populated largely by Swedes of color, is rationalized away by claims like those above—it's not about class, it's about culture. At the intersection of whiteness and class, white supremacy continues to hinder class solidarity and class prejudice continues to hinder antiracist understanding.

Swedes aren't the only ones clinging to a myth of an impossibly broad middle class. Roediger argues that in the past thirty years, the rhetoric of "saving the middle class" has shifted political language rightward in the United States, and "sidelined meaningful discussions of justice in terms of both class and race."[22] Since the 1990s, appeals to the middle class have become common currency in US electoral politics and thus to politics as many US Americans understand it as a whole. Appeals to the middle class are generally couched in an implicit "white" prefix: the rhetorical "middle class" is abstracted from white voters, who are believed to oppose unions, racial justice, welfare, and other too liberal or radical steps. While neoliberal reforms, financial crises, rising debt as well as wealth and income inequality, and deindustrialization have contributed to an increasingly precarious class structure in the United States, appeals to saving the middle class have continued unabated, supplemented in the past half decade with appeals to the "white working class" and its "economic anxiety."

News media helped bring the "white working class" into the spotlight, staging innumerable interviews with Trump voters who supposedly represented this demographic to air their grievances and fears. Tressie McMillan Cottom describes the framing of Trump voters as "losers" of "economic opportunities, financial security, identity, [and] gender supremacy": "People ate up the idea of Trump voters as losers. It is empathetic and, perhaps more importantly given how white and elite is the media profession, confirmation bias."[23] Nonwhite workers largely remained safely out of view, as did many class interests that are common across racial lines. Also safely ignored were others who were not involved in electoral politics and workers who support the things "white working-class" people supposedly oppose; for instance, 2019 AFL-CIO polling indicated that 40 percent of the white noncollege electorate was Democratic or Democratic leaning, 80 percent supported Black Lives Matter, and 82 percent opposed Trump's border wall.[24] Appeals to the middle or white working classes then appear as an appeal to invest in whiteness, and the talk of "economic anxiety" as a way to center white people's concerns about the ravages of neoliberal capitalism with the blame placed on nonwhite people. What emerges from this picture is a complex of apologetics for racism and support of white supremacy.

The turn to the white working class was not a US-exclusive phenomenon. Recent developments in Swedish political rhetoric have already been discussed. Similar changes occurred in the United Kingdom, with special fervor surrounding the Brexit vote, but in place long before. Reni Eddo-Lodge succinctly summarizes how the phrase "*white working class* plays into the rhetoric of the far right":

> Affixing the word "white" to the phrase "working class" suggests that these people face structural disadvantage because they are white, rather than because they are working class. These are newly regurgitated fears about white victimhood, fears that suggest that the real recipients of racism are white people, that this reverse racism happens because of the unfair "special treatment" that black people receive.[25]

In France, where immigrants and nonwhites in the *banlieues* (suburbs) are blamed for social ills in ways reminiscent of Sweden, the United States, and the United Kingdom, the whiteness of 2018's Yellow Vest protests is impossible to miss. A populist movement that emerged in rural France in protest of a new green tax on fuel, Yellow Vests soon attracted others who wanted to protest what they viewed as slipping standards of living. The Yellow Vests caused chaos and destruction, particularly in Paris, but were met with far less resistance than French people of color have during their own protests or possibly their daily lives. Most of them probably knew they would. The expectation is often that white violence will be treated with sympathy and understanding. A participant in the Washington, DC, Capitol siege in January 2021 encapsulated the presumption of liberty to violently express white grievances when she said, "This is not America. . . . They're shooting at us. They're supposed to shoot BLM, but they're shooting the patriots."[26]

Whiteness and Gender

Whiteness has long been associated with beauty, from the classicist valorization of the perceived whiteness of Greek and Roman statuary to the celebration of the white slave's supposed beauty in nineteenth-century odalisques to contemporary beauty standards. George M. Fredrickson notes that "aesthetic prejudice may have been more central to the negative assessments of non-Europeans and Jews in the eighteenth century than the tentative and ambiguous verdict of science about their intellectual capacities."[27] For centuries, white womanhood has been figured as unmatched beauty and untarnished morality. The continuing privileging of white beauty can be seen in consumer markets. Skin-lightening products are common around the world. According to the World Health Organization, "Beauty standards promoted by media, advertising and marketing reinforce the bias that lighter skin tone is more desirable than darker skin."[28] This idea is also commonly known as colorism and frequently has roots in colonial white supremacy. Skin lightening is a booming market, and such products are widely used in many African, Asian, and Caribbean countries as well as by darker-skinned populations in Europe and North America. They are potentially dangerous as well; many skin-lightening products contain dangerous levels of mercury.

On the flip side of this promotion of white supremacy–born colorism, the beauty product market for people of color is generally limited. Women of color have often had to provide what white-dominated beauty markets won't, from Madam C. J. Walker's early 1900s efforts to produce hair care products that took into account Black women's health needs (albeit based on white-centered beauty standards) to Rihanna's Fenty makeup line, launched in 2017 with the tagline "beauty for all," which introduced a range of cosmetics that allowed many women of color to match their own skin for the first time. The naturalized equation of "nude" or "skin" tones with traditionally white-identified shades is not limited to beauty products. Recent years have seen critiques of the whiteness of "flesh-colored" adhesive bandages to ballet pointe shoes, which dancers of color have long been forced to paint to match their skin. The latter is a symptom of who is considered to belong in ballet, and the former of who is considered human without racialized qualification.

The above exemplifies racialized gender norms and experiences, but gendered notions of whiteness and white notions of gender have many other effects and expressions. Different societies have different hegemonic or emphasized gender formations, and like any social formation, gender expectations and norms change over time. Emphasized white femininity tends to focus on the need for women to conform to men's needs and desires, and support male authority and power. It is also often understood to be aspirational and exclusive, and defined against Other femininities and masculinities. In the United States, for example, "new immigrants" in the pre–World War II years could be viewed as "oriental," which carried racialized connotations of "sensual abandon, lack of beauty, and unfitness for citizenship" that were associated with colonial stereotypes about Asians. Many policed their appearance accordingly (including by hair straightening and skin lightening, which have also been common among Black US Americans), while their sexuality was literally and figuratively policed; there was a widespread perception that prostitution was a new immigrant "racial" problem frequently connected in white public discourse to popular ideas about Asians. Immigrant women were expected to keep a tidy, white house, in line with classed and raced norms about what was suitably "American," and if they didn't (or couldn't), their Americanization or racial characteristics could be found wanting.[29] For groups like Jewish Americans, encounters with white majority society's gender norms inspired the creation of several Jewish gender stereotypes that rested on women's ability to either live up to emphasized white femininity or, later, embody it too well.[30]

Common to US American history is the juxtaposition of white women's vulnerability to Black men's supposed predatory nature, famously dramatized in 1915 in the cinematic celebration of the Ku Klux Klan, *Birth of a Nation*. In Sweden, as elsewhere in Europe, proper femininity was frequently juxtaposed against Romani women, who particularly during the nineteenth century were figured as seductive and sexually aggressive. Romani men were, and continue to be, portrayed instead as sexually predatory. Anti-Semitic propaganda also often figured Jewish men as a threat to white women. Many of these stereotypes are still in wide circulation. They are largely applied to other groups—especially Asian ones—but still serve to police white and nonwhite femininities and masculinities.

In Sweden, where hegemonic gender norms have shifted from patriarchal to officially feminist, gender equality is now framed as a defining Swedish trait, and often juxtaposed against "honor violence," patriarchal family structures, and other dangers to women figured as ingrained in immigrant cultures.

These predatory images have usually been used to motivate rhetorical and physical "retribution" to protect or free women. Foregrounding the issue of white feminism, cultural critic Mikki Kendall writes about Rebecca Latimer Felton, the first woman to serve in the US Senate (in 1922) and a supporter of lynching: "The fight of white women at that point was more about their freedom to oppress equally than it was about freeing all women from oppression." Felton's support of lynching was "rooted in the construction of white women as idealized archetypes of civilization that needed protection from the mythical sexuality of black men—a claim of violence that served to legitimize racist and imperialist actions before, during, and after Jim Crow."[31]

Felton's rhetoric and the use of women's vulnerability to justify racialized violence had a long history already in the early 1900s, and it has not gone away. White men and women continue to weaponize "white femininity to activate systems of racial terror against black men."[32] Today it is common for white women to call the police on Black men on spurious grounds, frequently with the knowledge that in the United States, policing as an institution is hostile to Black men.

Antimiscegenation laws and racially differentiated sentencing have been based on assumptions similar to Felton's, and attitudes like them can be found in contemporary constructions of rape, honor killings, and other gendered violence as being more prevalent as well as "worse" in Southeast Asia, the Middle East–North Africa, or segregated areas of so-called Western countries than they are in "Western," white spaces. Indeed, while much is currently different, attitudes of this type can be seen in the gendered rhetoric surrounding the so-called war on terror.[33] White feminist concern for Muslim women has been voiced in such disparate channels as former first lady Laura Bush's campaign to bring "civilization" to Afghan women and *X-Men* comics about the Muslim character Dust. This version of the "white woman's burden" has served to rationalize US American and other military presence in the Middle Eastern–North African, Central Asian, and South Asian regions, and justify surveillance, political and legal control, and violence elsewhere. The starting point for much of this discourse figures Muslims as Other to enlightened, liberated whiteness. Meanwhile, Muslim feminists in many countries have expressed their opposition to the hubris and lack of understanding betokened by simplistic claims about Muslim women needing to be "saved," based in Western and Islamophobic understandings of Islam and Islamicate contexts—ideas that can make their own struggles more difficult.[34]

Such Othering and rationalization of violence also accompany the prevalent self-understanding of Sweden as a feminist country. In a roundabout way, this understanding inspired a group calling itself the Soldiers of Odin—after a Finnish group founded in 2015 by a man with a clear neo-Nazi ideology to keep Finland white—to "patrol" Swedish streets chiefly in 2016–2017 and keep "its" Swedish (read white) women and children safe. Many members of this "law-and-order" group were themselves violent offenders, with violence against women on their records. The patrols led to violent altercations and physical abuse on several occasions. A journalistic exposé revealed a deeply sexist and racist environment, suggesting that the group's purpose was less to protect women than it was to protect whiteness from what they saw as its Others; after all, white violence was at the heart of the Soldiers of Odin's mission.[35] Engaging in a sort of sympathetic "white working-class" rhetoric, the reporters also noted that the group members aren't powerful people but instead unskilled laborers, truck drivers, nursing assistants, unemployed, or on long-term sick leave. The members, we're told, are looking for belonging and meaning. They're humanized and they allow themselves to be individualized in ways that nonwhite occupants of the same socioeconomic positions seldom are in white framings; the Soldiers of Odin's shattered expectations for life are presented as grounds for sympathy, even as they essentialize, pathologize, and racialize their Others with similar experiences.

These examples point to two important contemporary gendered intersections of whiteness: white feminism and the "crisis" of white masculinity. As scholar-activist Vron Ware observes, being (or being thought of as) white and female is to be (or be considered) part of a racialized, gendered category.[36] While being against one form of oppression (sexism) includes the possibility of being against another (here, racism), it nonetheless doesn't automatically lead to it. Many nineteenth- and twentieth-century women's movements, for instance, tended to have a limited conception of what constituted "universal suffrage" or which women were to be liberated, struggling as they usually did to win white women the vote or mobility without considering the oppressions that would keep women of color from reaping the fruits of the struggle.

Cast in a neoliberal garb today, white feminism focuses on individual advancement and opportunity, and frequently requires the exploitation of other women and marginalized groups, particularly people of color and people of marginalized genders or sexualities. It is, in author Koa Beck's definition,

> a type of feminism that takes up the politics of power without questioning them—by replicating

patterns of white supremacy, capitalistic greed, corporate ascension, inhumane labor practices, and exploitation, and deeming it empowering for women to practice these tenets as men always have. . . . The relentless optimization of the self often means that systemic and institutionalized barriers, to parental leave, to equal pay, to healthcare, to citizenship, to affordable childcare, to fair labor practices, are reframed as personal problems rather than collective disenfranchisement.[37]

The goal of this white feminism isn't to change or dismantle the power structures that oppress women, whether capitalism, patriarchy, or racism, but rather to succeed within them. The gains in professionalization and access to the workplace that are celebrated as feminist victories have largely benefited white women, who generally manage to project an image of progress by exploiting the labor of women of color that allows them to advance their careers. In Sweden, gender equality legislation in conjunction with tax reductions for housework and domestic labor costs in effect lets white women advance in the workplace on the backs of nonwhite women.[38] Nevertheless, the story of white feminism can also attract women of color, who hope that if they work hard enough, they can reap the same rewards. This isn't impossible, but the classed and racialized frames that guide white feminism might make it a more difficult proposition; white feminism centers white, middle-class realities, obstacles, and literacies, and ultimately works to reaffirm a white supremacy more inclusive of white women.

White men have rarely had to struggle for a seat at the white supremacist table. In the so-called West, ours has typically been the defining starting point of human existence, figured as the universal subject position from which other subject positions differ—the ground against which other identities are figured, to return to the language of the introduction. The term "hegemonic masculinity" was coined by sociologist Raewyn Connell in 1982 and has been a recurring theme of her work since.[39] Hegemonic masculinity is used to describe the most dominant and socially attractive form of masculinity in a given context at a given time, defined against other forms of masculinity or gender identities, and in racial, sexual, and socioeconomic terms. In white supremacist societies, hegemonic masculinity is delineated through ideals such as being brave, assertive or even aggressive to an extent, and stoic in the face of challenges, threats, and problems, while displays of emotion or admitting weakness are discouraged. A "real man" cannot be too effeminate; a "real man" is more desirable than a woman in leadership positions, since women are "too emotional"; a "real man" knows what he wants and is willing to take it, but is not "savage" like Black or Muslim men are often claimed to be. Hegemonic masculinity doesn't reflect most white men's lived reality but instead provides a normative form of masculinity to aspire to.

What the Swedish reporters saw in the Soldiers of Odin is not unique. The increase in what sociologist Michael Kimmel calls "angry white men" in recent decades is tied to "aggrieved entitlement," "the sense that 'we,' the rightful heirs, . . . have had what is 'rightfully ours' taken away from us by 'them,' faceless, feckless government bureaucrats, and given to 'them,' undeserving minorities, immigrants, women, gays, and their ilk." Whiteness as property fosters certain expectations from life; so does maleness, which in a similar same sense might be considered a form of property. The relative cash value of white maleness are hard to dispute in many white-majority nations, but its public and psychological wages may have decreased somewhat. In the face of growing downward mobility along with increased racial and gender equality, many white men "circle the wagons" and try to roll back moves toward equality and equity, rather than look to the economic and political changes that may have made life worse for white men, although even more so for the less privileged. "The game has changed," as Kimmel puts it, "but instead of questioning the rules, they want to eliminate the other players."[40]

One way this aggrieved entitlement plays out is in so-called toxic masculinity, an aggressive masculinity that's dismissive of emotion and often puts strong emphasis on the idea central to the concept of "emphasized femininity": that women's primary role is to comply with men's sexual advances and desires. This is a particular hallmark of the incel, or involuntary celibate, rhetoric. The sense of entitlement that drives today's "crisis of white masculinity" is born out of raced and gendered privilege and expectations, but the troubles against which angry white men rage are more often classed; as already noted, scapegoating directs the blame away from the source and onto less powerful groups.[41] Aggrieved entitlement drives the mission of white male-dominated organizations like the Tea Party, Proud Boys, or Soldiers of Odin; it animates online movements like Gamergate or Comicsgate, where small moves toward diversity in popular culture fields are opposed as the erasure of white men; and it is at the heart of Trumpism and an ongoing shift of white male, European voters from traditional social democratic worker's and liberal middle-class parties to the ranks of right-wing populist parties.

Tied into the crisis of white masculinity, perhaps especially the growth of right-wing populist parties, are the changing demographics in much of the so-called West. The United States is projected to be a majority-minority nation by the mid-2040s, and much of Europe will soon have 25 to 35 percent non-Western and non-Christian populations.[42] Many groups connect these changes to the white genocide and Great Replacement conspiracy theories, and argue for different ways of rising to the supposed challenge. Historically and in the present, these fears are often coupled with a sexual dimension of raced gender. Earlier discussions have mentioned antimiscegenation and other marriage laws, antiabortion rhetoric, and the like. In more recent decades, these measures have been mostly replaced by "family-friendly" policies. This type of measure is frequently a racial project to support white supremacist racial formation. Richard Dyer writes that "race and gender are ineluctably intertwined, through the primacy of heterosexuality in reproducing the former and defining the latter."[43] For all the changes in racial, classed, and gendered structures that have been undertaken internationally in recent decades, the hegemonic aspirational ideal in much of the white West still remains the position most securely held, historically and today, by straight white men of means. It is still the backdrop against which other identities are discursively framed and socioeconomically positioned, and it is what angry white men strive to recuperate and white feminists strive to incorporate into.

Whiteness All the Way Down

The naturalization of whiteness in much of the so-called Western world remains firmly in place. In addition to the examples of medical racism already cited, people of color have a harder time being properly diagnosed for many illnesses, say, because many ways of seeing symptom expressions are tailored to white bodies. In addition to segregation that impacts people of color worldwide and the still deep-rooted legacies of redlining that make it more difficult for people of color in the United States to become homeowners, and thus access a main source of intergenerational wealth, many spaces worldwide are organized with whiteness firmly in mind. Gentrification and "urban renewal" often disproportionately impact and displace people of color, and in many places, people of color are reminded on an everyday basis of racism, colonialism, slavery, and white supremacist imperialism through the monuments and buildings named after perpetrators that remain a constant feature of many Western urban landscapes. The environment itself is deeply imprinted by whiteness, notably in the form of environmental racism, which promotes everything from the disproportionate placement of dangerous industries, facilities, and infrastructure in majority nonwhite areas to the unequally distributed impact of climate change.

Whiteness also rests at the core of common understandings of "religion," a term that was defined in a colonial situation on a white, European model and continues to be understood through that lens to this day. Schooling continues in many white supremacist societies to tell white history as if it were universal, breaking out and separating nonwhite histories as specialty subjects, rather than

Whiteness isn't natural,
it's learned.

indelible parts of national and international histories. The ways people speak is inflected with whiteness. In Australia in the early 1900s and the United States around the turn of that century, literacy tests were used in attempts to limit entry for undesirable immigrants. Often "white" forms of speech are valued higher than nonwhite ones, and white-sounding names are often a ticket to better opportunities on the job market or in social networks. Time and time again, new technologies or algorithms illustrate how deep naturalized whiteness and structural white supremacy truly runs, when report after report tells of new instances where racial bias has been hardwired, albeit frequently unconsciously, into the heart of new systems. But whiteness isn't natural, it's learned. Among the primary sites where whiteness is reproduced and taught to mass audiences is also a place where many perhaps would not think to look for it.

POPULAR WHITENESS

"Race" does not refer to naturally occurring phenomena but rather socially and politically constructed subject positions that people subscribe to or are ascribed. No understanding of race gains or can maintain salience or meaning outside language. Race must be actively kept alive in the minds of those who view it as a social fact. In the words of Eduardo Bonilla-Silva, racial domination necessitates "something like a grammar to normalize the standards of white supremacy as *the* standards for all sorts of everyday transactions rendering domination almost invisible."[1] Building on racial ideology, this changing racial grammar guides what can be said about race and how, and what can be seen, felt, or understood about it. It is acquired through social interaction and communication.

This book has already included examples from popular culture. This is not only because popular culture is a useful way to illustrate how whiteness can function and as such make the structures discussed more concrete. Popular culture is itself also an important part of racial formation. As Michael Omi and Howard Winant write, hegemonic racial ideology has to be reinforced to last, "not only in state policies and court decisions, but in popular culture and everyday life as well."[2]

Popular culture is an important site for the reproduction and circulation of discourses and relations of power. It has historically contributed to the ordering and preservation of racial hierarchies, and continues to participate in shifting and normalizing codes of race and racial formation. Not only are its representations bounded by structures that inform what can and cannot be credibly said in any given racial formation, but they can serve to either uphold or challenge those limits. Popular culture, then, is a major site for the inscription and maintenance of white epistemologies of ignorance as well as attempts to oppose them. Popular culture is inseparable from whiteness as a structure of oppression and part of its inner workings.

It isn't possible here to discuss all the ways these struggles over meaning and structure take place. Such an overview would inevitably become too broad and shallow to say much. Rather, this chapter will focus on three main topics: white children's literature, white superhero fictions, and white sitcoms. These three were chosen for specific reasons: the first is connected to the earliest

Popular culture is a major site for the inscription and maintenance of white epistemologies of ignorance as well as attempts to oppose them.

stages of socialization, and thus to the emergence of racialized awareness and epistemic ignorance; the second because it is a currently dominant form of popular culture, presented as being about questions of good and evil, and framed by as well as framing a racialized morality; and the third because while it is presented as escapism, recently often in explicit disavowal of any meaning at all ("shows about nothing"), it has historically effected racial segregation through its broadcasts and scheduling.

"Gentle Doses of Racism": White Children's Literature

Children's literature in the West is pervasively white. It has been for a long time. It is perhaps not difficult to consider that, say, children's literature in Victorian Britain or colonial France wore white supremacy and racist stereotypes on their sleeves. It may also be easy to credit that more recent works of no less "classic" children's fiction reproduce racist and white supremacist structures, such as the *Pippi Longstocking* stories (1945–) by Swedish author Astrid Lindgren (1907–2002). Lindgren's use of the N-word in one story caused controversy in Sweden and abroad around the beginning of the 2010s, and a revised version that excised the word was published. Lindgren herself said in 1970 that she would not have used the word if she had written the story then instead of decades earlier.

Neither then nor more recently was there much discussion of the story's clear hierarchization of white and nonwhite, or romanticization of colonialism. It is this structural dimension, rather than word choices, that preoccupies many academic critiques of the state of children's literature today. However much has changed since Pippi first appeared, much remains the same.

Children's literature scholar Ebony Elizabeth Thomas writes about a "diversity gap" in children's publishing manifest in a lack of representation of characters of color as well as in stereotyping, caricature, and marginalization, and largely white authorship even of books with more diverse representation.[3] The Cooperative Children's Book Center at the University of Wisconsin at Madison collects and publishes statistics on diversity in US American children's literature regularly. According to the 2018 statistics, white characters constitute about half of those represented in children's books. Animals and other nonhuman figures account for another 27 percent. The remaining 23 percent are broken down into the categories "African/African American" (10 percent), "Asian Pacific Islander/Asian Pacific American" (7 percent), "Latinx" (5 percent), and "American Indians/First Nations" (1 percent). An illustrated representation of these statistics by library and information science scholar Sarah Park Dahlen and artist David Huyck (see figure 2) puts them in further context: they portray white characters in multidimensional ways,

Figure 2 Sarah Park Dahlen and artist David Huyck's visualization of children's literature data, created in consultation with Edith Campbell, Molly Beth Griffin, K. T. Horning, Debbie Reese, Ebony Elizabeth Thomas, and Madeline Tyner, with statistics compiled by the Cooperative Children's Book Center, School of Education, University of Wisconsin at Madison. Released for use under a Creative Commons Attribution-ShareAlike 4.0 International (CC BY-SA 4.0 license). https://readingspark.wordpress.com/2019/06/19/picture-this-diversity-in-childrens-books-2018-infographic.

exemplified by a variety of mirrors showing different reflections and placed in a vivid setting, while characters of color are represented by a series of successively shrinking cracked mirrors placed on increasingly drab backgrounds. The cracks are meant to illustrate how children's literature continues to misrepresent underrepresented communities.

The production side of the equation, who tells stories to children, was even less diverse, as it had been before; in 2015, for example, out of the 42 books listed with Native American characters, three had been written by Native writers. The rest were "full of stereotype, bias, and factual errors."[4] A similar situation obtained in 2018 in the United Kingdom, although there it was even easier for a reader of color to find a story about an animal or inanimate object than a person who resembles them.[5]

Likewise, while Sweden is sometimes viewed as a leading country in children's literature, its diversity is poorly reflected in the industry and its input. In 2013, when Sweden was the "guest of honor" at the International Children's Book Fair in Bologna, Italy, all 31 illustrators showcased were white. Like many other sectors of Swedish public life, white representation was overwhelming, and the country's multicultural reality was not reflected in its self-representation to the world. A report from the Swedish Institute for Children's Literature that samples publications from 2018 notes that Swedish children's literature is becoming more diverse. The report includes a survey of picture books produced in Sweden or published in Swedish translation that shows that people of color appear in 44 percent of the books studied, in 123 Swedish books and 45 non-Swedish ones. People of color have active roles in 67 of these books and leading roles in 35. Twenty-six of the latter category are of Swedish origin and 9 appear in non-Swedish books.[6]

This appears to be an active attempt to diversify, but skin color doesn't factor into the storytelling. What this means is explained further in a general discussion of "bodily norms" in picture books:

> In Sara Lövenstam and Per Gustavsson's *Under Mattan* [Under the rug] for example, the visual narrative presents an Indian [South Asia] origin but the text doesn't thematically address it. The same strategy appears in Jesper Lundqvist and Marcus-Gunnar Petterson's *Rädslorna* [The fears] where a dark-skinned man grapples with being too comfortable with his fears, but his origin isn't communicated.[7]

Diversity in Swedish picture books thus seems to follow the broader national approach to race: it is color-blind, and suggests that limited inclusion may on its own counter a long-standing structure of exclusion along with its underlying reasons and effects.

In addition to a "diversity gap," Thomas points to an "imagination gap," in part caused by the lack of diversity in representations of childhood and teen life in children's literature and other media. "When youth grow up without seeing diverse images in the mirrors, windows, and doors of children's and young adult literature, they are confined to single stories about the world around them and, ultimately, the development of their imagination is affected." Thomas suggests that this gap adversely affects some kids and teens of color's desire to read. Maybe it's not so much that they don't want to read but rather that those on the production side of children's literature and similar media "haven't thought very much about the racialized mirrors, windows, and doors that are in the books we offer them to read."[8]

This imagination gap can have serious consequences for children racialized as white and nonwhite. Philosopher Brynn F. Welsh writes that "the pervasive whiteness of children's literature contributes to the cultivation of racial biases and stereotypes, impedes the cultivation of compassion for others, and renders valuable goods less accessible to children of color than to white children."[9] Representations encountered early in a child's development can shape understandings of the world and leave lasting impressions. They can help form compassion for others, or foster stereotypes and racial bias. Reading is part of children's moral development and the formation of a "theory of mind." It helps form emotional investment in the well-being of others, and can foster understandings of sameness and difference, and even promote connection across differences. The continuing whiteness of children's literature can mean that children do not often see, think about, or become invested in characters of color.

Such a manufactured lack of understanding of and empathy for nonwhite people can be seen in instances like the above-mentioned controversy surrounding Pippi. Many white Swedes have rushed to defend Pippi and other historical racist representations by claiming that "it was different back then, not like today—this type of talk was acceptable!" It certainly was, for white people. But it was acceptable because white people had normalized racism, and viewed dehumanizing stereotypes and colonial celebration as normal. Pointing to the acceptability of racist imagery in the past only reaffirms old racist narratives and rationalizations. The experience and objections of the marginalized of the past are eliminated from the historical record. This type of argument then illustrates a way of forming and maintaining white epistemological ignorance: on the one hand, it manufactures a detached, historical gaze and places it over the supposedly presentist, overly emotional gaze of detractors; on the other hand, it positions the present as a more enlightened, less racist age.

What is absent from the page is also important: one cannot empathize with someone one can't imagine as having an inner life. Seeing an all-white world with no or only a few people of color naturalizes whiteness as the norm. While many of the racist caricatures or stereotypes of old are gone, new ones have taken their place, and seeing people of color playing only a few roles (e. g., civil rights activist, athlete, or musician) perpetuates common perceptions of acceptable fields of activity and life, which creates an understanding of the world based on exclusionary, historically rooted social, cultural, and economic boundaries. Other stereotypes appear in new and still-available older works, and shape people's understanding of what is an acceptable racial representation of "Asians," "Africans," "Indians," or other groups. Calls for more diverse representation often meet with resistance, however. A common critique is that so-called forced diversity infantilizes people of color. One frequent claim is that it's insulting to suggest that people of color can't imagine themselves in the shoes of white characters. That would indeed be an insulting argument, but it's a distortion. More commonly, the point is that people of color *have* to do the extra work of imagining themselves or people who look like them in the place of white characters if they want to engage with the fantasy. As one British reader of children's literature said, "Most of the people I pictured were white because in most of the stories I read there are no black people."[10]

Thus it is easy to conclude that whatever else may have changed, and despite the growing calls for diversity on the children's literature page and in the industry, educator Nancy Larrick's 1965 critique of the "all-white world of children's books" still applies to a large segment of the industry: "Although his [sic] white skin makes him one of the world's minorities, the white child learns from his books that he is the kingfish. There seems little chance of developing the humility so urgently needed for world cooperation, instead of world conflict, as long as our children are brought up on gentle doses of racism through their books."[11] It bears repeating: race isn't a natural or neutral category. It is made. Human beings are socialized into seeing or not seeing ourselves as raced beings. Children's literature is a significant site of this socialization. In superdiverse countries like Sweden or the United States, which will soon be a majority-minority country, the continuing pervasiveness of whiteness marks out children's literature—and many other cultural fields—as contributing to a truly "invented delusional world, a racial fantasyland" that only sets up future generations of white children for white fragility when they are faced with their own racialized position, and white rage when they feel like the world isn't living up to what it's promised them.[12]

"With Great Power": White Superheroes

A persistent cliché holds that "comics aren't just for kids anymore." Whether they ever were is a question for somewhere else, but the long-standing association of superheroes with children is fast becoming untenable; the current popular cultural moment is dominated by superheroes. "Superheroes" refers here to the type of character most associated with Marvel and DC Comic's transmedia ventures—characters with powers, intellects, skill sets, or bank balances that can only be described as superhuman, and who fight for an ill-defined "good" or "justice." Four of the top-grossing movies in 2019 were superhero themed, and six out of ten were the previous year. Streaming video on demand platforms are brimming with superhero offerings, from DC's Arrowverse to Marvel shows like *Daredevil*, *Luke Cage*, *Runaways*, and *Cloak & Dagger*, to other fare like *Heroes*, *Jupiter's Children*, or *The Boys*. Superhero comic books continue to be produced, as do digital and analog games as well as innumerable superhero-branded consumer products.

There are exceptions, perhaps most famously the Black-led *Black Panther* movie (2018), but generally this broad-based consumer culture centers on whiteness. Superheroes have always been a largely US American phenomenon, but they are becoming increasingly international. Production elsewhere has mostly failed to find an audience, however, and when it has been moderately successful, whiteness-centered tropes, conventions, and assumptions have often been reproduced. Bound by the logic of mass-market appeal, superhero stories continue to be produced using the "racial grammar" of US racial formation, primarily for an imagined audience of racially unmarked—that is to say, white—consumers. The end product usually seems to operate from the assumption that white faces, bodies, and experiences can best reflect universal standards and expectations. This is sometimes made explicit. In 2009, for example, Marvel editor Tom Brevoort said that there are certainly readers within the white male demographic "who are interested in a wide assortment of characters of diverse ethnicities and backgrounds." In a framing that suggested that whiteness is universally appealing, he claimed that "whenever your leads are white American males, you've got a better chance of reaching more people overall."[13] This is an explicit acquiescence to white habitus, and a reproduction of a long history of white male dominance in US and global representation.[14]

The whiteness of this type of superhero has deep roots. If Superman is the founding figure of the genre, as is often claimed, then whiteness was inscribed in 1938 at the moment of foundation. While the early Superman's whiteness was framed as more inclusive than traditional WASP whiteness, it was nevertheless exclusive; created by two young Jewish American men, Superman's stories seem to attempt to counter the push of US American anti-Semitism and emphasize the pull of integration. Superman's earliest years (1938–1941) exclude people of color, other than to highlight their difference from white ethnic US Americans, and employ raced gender stereotypes to frame "proper," white femininity as superior to "improper," ethnic femininities.[15] Cartoonist Will Eisner's Spirit similarly figured whiteness as more inclusive of ethnic difference from his first appearance in June 1940, using racial caricature to do so. The Spirit's sidekick, Ebony White, was a blackface caricature who embodied many anti-Black stereotypes in appearance, word, and deed. Along with a whole supporting cast of similarly drawn blackface figures, Ebony helped create a world in which Blackness was the true measure of difference, marking minor ethnic differences as less significant. Finally, the superpatriotic, blond, and blue-eyed Steve Rogers, Captain America, introduced in early 1941, exemplified the understanding of World War II as a racial war by fighting enemies represented along racial lines: Nazis were depicted with their humanity intact, while Japanese foes were frequently turned into claw-fingered and fanged racial grotesques.

While the overt racism of these years has dampened over the decades, it would take until the 1960s before superheroes of color gained a small foothold. The number of superheroes of color has remained low. When a new nonwhite superhero appears, they are generally turned into a media event. Minority characters are often expected to represent entire demographics, which is never an expectation of white characters. Many of these characters quickly recede into the margin or background, however, leaving many groups without even token representation among superheroes. Nevertheless, the number of nonwhite superhero characters is slowly growing.

Whether one views this as progress or cynical attempts by corporations to survive in times of change and upheaval, the archetypal image of the superhero remains the same as it has always been: a muscular white man. Most superheroes that diverge from this model and other hegemonic identity formations are marked as different in marketing and by critics. There are Black, female, Muslim, and LGBTQIA2S+ superheroes, for example, but their superherodom is typically marked in the stories as well. This is perhaps most clear in the Black superheroes that started appearing in the late 1960s and the following years whose superhero aliases racialized them from the outset, such as Black Panther (1966), Black Goliath (1973), and Black Lightning (1977).[16] Others, like Luke Cage (1972) or Shang-Chi (1973), were introduced to capitalize on the popularity of blaxploitation or martial arts movies, but written from within a white racial frame and frequently employing stereotypes. In some cases, high-profile Black-coded characters like the *X-Men*'s Storm have instead been drawn and characterized based on Eurocentric standards of beauty and femininity. Social psychologist Kenneth Ghee even describes many white-created, Black-coded superheroes as "white heroes in Black face," noting that most such characters exist in otherwise Eurocentric, white worlds, and work to support whiteness-centered causes and goals.[17]

Generally it is white men who can be simply superheroes without further qualification. To the extent that superhero stories are power fantasies, then, they are perhaps most often fantasies of white (male) power. This is unsurprising since superhero narratives—at least from the more established publishers—continue largely to be created by white men, even when they tell stories about characters of color. There is also evidence that whiteness is a factor in superhero stories' reception. Several scholars have discussed vocal contingents of white readers' opposition to Black superheroes; the mere presence of a Black superhero is too political or unrealistic for some readers.[18] As scholar Consuela Francis notes, a common white "readers' assumption [is] that black equals political and that political equals bad or, at least, unentertaining art."[19] Other readers see the lack of diversity and overwhelming whiteness of superhero worlds as equally political and problematic. Unsatisfied with what he saw in comics and the lack of characters for Black readers to identify with, Ghee created a superhero in 2010 meant to transcend those patterns. Similarly, the editors of the 2009 *Asian American Superhero Anthology* collected stories by Asian American creators, featuring Asian American characters, to make up for the lack of Asian American superheroes in the bigger publishers' outputs, and as the first page of the anthology testifies to, with an array of different stereotypical characters, to challenge prejudices about Asian Americans.[20] And in 2011, comic maker Supreet Singh Manchanda started working on his Super Sikh character, citing issues with the proliferation of superhero movies: "Would you believe all these Marvel comic characters that are being made into movies? . . . They're more than 50 years old, they're very two dimensional, there's very little cultural nuance to them, they're all white."[21]

Superhero fictions generally tend to be reactive and even reactionary. What superheroes fight for varies, as does who they fight. But a common denominator is that often the struggle is as much to preserve society as it is against interlopers who advocate radical change. Supervillains can give voice to exaggerated and brutal versions of common social critiques, giving to them a dangerous edge that disqualifies the criticism from the outset. This means that what is at stake in superhero battles is usually a status quo founded on white supremacy. Sometimes this is extensively euphemized. At other times it is manifest on the page, as in the *Captain America* story arc "The Extremists" published shortly after 9/11. Here, Captain America was made to fight Redpath (another racialized alias), a Native American character whose violent uprising was explicitly framed as revenge for white settler colonialism; in a climactic scene, Captain America is dramatically made to scream that he is "*sick*—of *people*—trashing this country!"[22] (See figures 3 and 4.) In the course of "The Extremists," a critique of white supremacy, depicted as a failure to live up to the nation's "founding ideals," is hyperbolically transformed into a battle to put down an anti–US American rebellion. Whether framed as clearly as this or not, the threat to white supremacy is almost always beaten back in superhero narratives and the (white) social order is restored.

Indeed, critiques of racial formation and white supremacy remain rare in superhero fictions. While there are exceptions, superhero fictions' engagements with race generally uphold whiteness even while making gestures toward diversity. English professor Marc Singer looks at a particularly clear example from a 1976 issue of a *Legion of Super-Heroes* comic of how superhero stories frequently make recourse to "color blindness" (discussed more in the next chapter).

In the comics, the Legion was often presented with a multicultural framing. Many of its members were aliens and as such obviously different from the mostly white humans of earth in the thirtieth century. This alien difference was sometimes used to stand in for real-world forms of difference from normative whiteness. When, two decades into the *Legion*'s publication history, however, a Black-coded superhero was finally offered membership, one Legionnaire tells him that "when it comes to race, we're color-blind! Blue skin, yellow skin, green skin . . . we're

Figure 3 The villainous Redpath [*sic*] expresses the critique of supremacy that signals his villainy. In *Captain America* 4, no. 8 (March 2002). © Marvel 2016.

Figure 4 Captain America models the "proper" response to resistance against white supremacy. In *Captain America* 4, no. 9 (April 2003). © Marvel 2016.

brothers and sisters . . . united in the name of justice everywhere!" Singer notes that "the Legionnaires cite their own skin colors as proof of their inclusivity. Significantly, no race is assigned to the first character in the tableau, the white Superboy; even though he hails from an alien planet, his white skin normalizes him as not belonging to any 'race.'"[23]

The Legionnaires of color thus embody a common color-blind cliché: according to sociologist Ruth Frankenberg, phrasings like this, about how it doesn't matter whether a person is "black, green, yellow, or pink," or any other constellation of colors, can be understood as a strategy to avoid talking about race: "it shifts attention away from color differences that make a political difference by embedding meaningful differences among nonmeaningful ones."[24] Blackness, a racial formation with actual real-world effects, is equated with greenness or blueness, which are not social facts in the same way (Kentucky's famously blue-skinned Fugate family notwithstanding). Blackness is introduced only to be actively dismissed. Whiteness, on the other hand, remains invisible; even the green and blue aliens are coded as white, and the white-coded character is implicitly presented as raceless.[25]

A further dimension can be added to this equation. The *X-Men* franchise of superhero fictions has since its introduction in 1963 become increasingly framed around difference. The central trope, "mutantcy," is malleable, but has for decades been a biological metaphor: Marvel's mutants are people who through a genetic difference receive special powers. Because of this, they are sometimes hunted and despised. Mutantcy has been used in a variety of persecution narratives to stand in for Blackness, Jewishness, LGBTQIA2S+ identity, and more. The stories' activation of different identities has been strategic to make broad points about how oppression is bad, but commonly in a way that mixes real-world, socially meaningful difference with the floating signifier of mutantcy. Blackness, Jewishness, queerness, and so on, are only rarely addressed as politically salient, and almost always put on a level playing field with mutantcy. All of this has served to flatten all forms of oppression or sense of outsiderness, and conflate them. This works ultimately in favor of a largely white and male imagined readership, which is repeatedly invited to make the oppression and persecution of marginalized groups its own. Thus mutantcy tends to re-center whiteness even when it is meant to embody difference.

Further problematizing the equation of mutantcy with various forms of difference is the hard biological coding of the trope. Mutants *are* inherently different, no matter what group they stand in for in any given story line. Mutants *are* dangerous, and the repeated attempts by mutants to take over the world or destroy humankind motivate the various X-Men teams' struggle to police and patrol "evil" mutants, many of whom explicitly fight against oppression. The franchise was founded on the integrationist and respectability political idea that if mutants just work to show humans they aren't dangerous, humans will eventually accept them, and that has remained a central facet of most *X-Men* narratives over the decades. The recurring message is that mutant difference is only acceptable if it doesn't challenge the status quo; mutants who don't adhere to social norms or oppose oppressive structures must the defeated. Acceptance comes only to those who wait.

As a fictional character type, the superhero typically champions justice. But between the lines, its fight against amorphous "evil" appears conservative, rooted in as well as defending unequal and oppressive structures with all of its might. If superheroes are forces for "good," as is often taken for granted, an important follow-up question that is far more rarely asked is, Who are they good for, and who pays the price for their physical, rhetorical, and emotional violence?

Least Objectionable: White Sitcoms

In an installment of Aaron McGruder's *The Boondocks* comic strip (November 12, 1999), Jazmine Dubois asks Huey Freeman what Eurocentrism means. Huey responds that "it's when you eliminate the African perspective and marginalize or omit people of color—their contributions, their experiences, etc." When Jazmine still doesn't understand, Huey asks, "Do you ever watch '*Friends*'?" Jazmine says yes, and Huey delivers the punch line: "Then you understand."[26]

The joke has remained relevant. *Friends* (1994–2004) has achieved cult status and remains part of public life worldwide, and its whiteness is still a topic of discussion. But the underlying circumstances were not unique to *Friends*. NBC's vice president for audience measurement Paul L. Klein coined the phrase "least objectionable programming" in 1971, claiming that viewers tend to choose the least objectionable show available to them rather than seeking out something specific to watch. CBS was successful with television shows that appealed to a broader spectrum of viewers, targeting especially young adults, teens, and adolescents, while appealing to the "lowest common denominator." The network's "perennial success" inspired competitors to follow suit.[27] Much has changed since, such as assumptions about what is objectionable to whom, and what demographics are considered most desirable. There are now more networks and streaming platforms to choose from, and re-viewing older shows is easier. Nevertheless, pleasing the most viewers remains perhaps less important than offending the fewest. To this end, whiteness with its attendant Eurocentrism remains a dominant norm.

Thus while explicit discussions of race occur in white sitcoms, race is often a factor most notable in its absence.

Friends is a prominent example. Communications professor Phil Chidester has argued that "*Friends'* popularity is rooted not only in the program's value as a source of entertainment, but in its efforts to defend whiteness's hegemonic privilege in contemporary America." Since US American television has been and largely remains a white and frequently racially segregated field, social patterns are continuously reproduced in programs like *Friends*. As Chidester observes, "For those who are rarely confronted with racial difference in actual experience and who have come to expect media content that is likewise free of references to race, episodes of *Friends* ring true."[28]

Friends offers a sanitized worldview; its New York City is clean, free from any problems, and almost entirely white. The major exception is Joey, whose "rough" Italian American edges serve as a liminal marker of not-quite-whiteness often used to highlight "proper" behaviors by contrast. The show largely implies a presumed irrelevance of identity politics. Ethnoracial and sexual difference appears, but it generally serves to strengthen these boundaries. For instance, Ross's lesbian ex-wife is frequently the butt of homophobic jokes, and his nonwhite girlfriends, Julie and Charlie, are objects of racist jokes during their short tenures on the show. Otherwise, people of color are almost exclusively seen in minor, passing roles, generally couched in stereotypes. The main cast is a closed circle, a white enclave whose borders are rarely permeated. More than anything else, difference means disruption or distraction in *Friends*.

This wasn't always the case. Two of the first television sitcoms were adapted from radio comedies: *Amos 'n' Andy* (1951–1953) and *The Goldbergs* (1949–1956). The first, which was rooted in blackface minstrelsy, was canceled after two seasons amid criticisms from the National Association for the Advancement of Colored People, Black veterans, and other protesters. *The Goldbergs*, which employed ethnic Jewish stereotypes, lasted longer, in part because the ethnic references were gradually removed and the show was suburbanized for broader appeal.[29] More firmly white fare took their place, and the genre has remained largely segregated since. This segregation can be seen clearly in the emergence of a loose category of "Black sitcoms," as opposed to supposedly "universal" white ones. The former have typically been scheduled on the basis of cast rather than content, using race as a determiner of appeal. These practices "have reinforce[d] the notion that skin color delimits style, aesthetics, and narrative interests, and that actors with Black skin are of no concern to White audiences."[30]

A telling example of such practices and their consequences can be seen in the story of *Living Single* (1993–1998), which adds an important nuance to McGruder's joke above. Premiering a year before *Friends*, *Living Single* is so similar in format to *Friends* that it's highly likely the later television show built off the earlier, especially since both were produced by the same company. *Living Single*'s main cast consisted of Black actors, and the show portrayed a more diverse image of New York City. But *Living Single* was marketed mainly to Black audiences while the all-white *Friends* was pushed in most available channels to all potential audiences. The shows' respective legacies reflect this racial disparity. While white audiences were likely to never hear of the successful and popular *Living Single*, Black audiences—or any other audience, whether in the United States or many foreign markets—were unlikely to miss *Friends*.

Even though they've been marginalized from the wider culture, Black sitcoms have nevertheless often had to "walk a thin line to attract White Americans while not alienating African Americans."[31] The middle-class construct and avoidance of racism in *The Cosby Show* (1984–1992) exemplify this least objectionable framing.[32] The emergence of cable channels like Fox, WB, and UPN after the late 1980s inspired further segregation. The newcomers catered to Black audiences while the established networks developed more white-centered shows. In either case, most sitcoms "airing throughout the 1990s were produced by Whites, written by predominantly White writing teams, who worked under the supervision of White network executives, who sold advertising time to White advertising agents, who represented corporations managed by Whites."[33]

White sitcoms, for their part, have followed some general trends. Starting early in television history many programs showcased vaguely ethnic, white, working-class people learning to appreciate the "American dream" along with the ideals of consumption and credit, which continued into shows like *Roseanne* (1988–1997, 2018). Many white 1970s' sitcoms were more political, discussing matters of race and gender in a period where white identity politics were becoming more salient, but rarely to the point of critiquing whiteness. By the 1990s, so-called shows about nothing successfully voided much of this earlier political messaging in favor of a supposedly depoliticized rhetoric.[34] According to film and media scholar Taylor Nygaard and television scholar Jorie Lagerwey, we are currently in a cycle of "horrible white people" comedies that are dressed in the trappings of "quality" TV, rooted in middle-class taste cultures, and address a sense of white precarity. Again, the target audience is primarily white:

> This cycle reflects Peak TV's insatiable demand
> for and attempt to use those quality aesthetics to
> appeal to ever-diminishing audiences of White,
> relatively affluent, tech-savvy, educated, urban
> viewers described by traditional discourses of quality

audiences. . . . Those White consumers' inflated importance to a still-dominant cultural force [TV] thus becomes one of the cultural structures that maintain and support White supremacy.[35]

This is an international matter. Sitcoms are big US American and UK exports. Audiences in other nations might not understand the contextually rooted differences between white and Black sitcoms, and scheduling and marketing may not adhere to the same segregating principles, but the racial grammar of the genre carries over. Indeed, the horrible white people era has, more than earlier ones, fostered a transnational collective identity based on shared taste cultures and feelings of white precarity. Following the rise of streaming video on demand, international cofinancing has become more common, and the audience address has focused less on nationality and more on transnational racial and class-based affinities.[36]

In their whiteness, sitcoms frequently build on the racial grammar of everyday life in the United States, United Kingdom, or other country of production. The common lack of discussions of race as a social issue often makes white sitcoms appear color-blind. Yet race has been and continues to be a common implicit factor. Nonwhite characters are few and far between not only in *Friends* but also in other "classics" of the genre like *Seinfeld* (1989–1998), *Cheers* (1982–1993), or *Everybody Loves Raymond*

(1996–2005). Newer programs, like *Emily in Paris* (2020–), continue this symbolic erasure, while others, such as *Dear White People* (2017–2021) or *Insecure* (2016–2021), press against the continuing tide of whiteness.[37] This is not accidental. Sitcoms, like all popular entertainments, perform an ideological function. They don't simply reflect social realities or experiences; they order and work on them in relation to social concerns and cultural changes. They usually, as *Friends* did, "shape and reinforce both white audiences' perceptions of the racialized Other and of marginalized audience members' perceptions of themselves as raced beings," and through that help maintain or reinforce white supremacy.[38] By their appeals to whiteness, they can construct an imagined community. The institutions producing the programs further reinforce the social structures of white supremacy by centering as well as prioritizing the concerns and tastes of ever-smaller, more clearly race- and class-defined audiences that are considered more desirable in the halls of television power.

Between 2017 and 2019, comedies made up roughly one-third to two-fifths of US American television. Overall, recent developments have seen increasing diversity in casting and lead roles, and the slow diversification of writers' rooms.[39] Even though streaming giants like Netflix continue to position themselves as progressive and diverse, however, people of color remain significantly underrepresented in all forms of US American television.

Similar circumstances apply for people of color in the UK television industry, where (often supporting) on-screen roles are more common than off-screen ones.[40] Some Black British sitcom creators have opted to sidestep traditional channels to avoid questions about whether they "can make white people laugh."[41] The adage that the more things change, the more they stay the same comes to mind.

Indeed, media studies professor Amanda Dyanne Lotz wrote in the early 2000s that the then-recent US American commentary and campaigns had "emphasized the relative insignificance of gains in diversity in front of the camera if similar gains are not made in the creative decision-making and executive structure."[42] The 2020 "Hollywood Diversity Report" produced by the University of California at Los Angeles echoes this sentiment almost exactly:

> The meaningful progress this report documents in the television sector has largely occurred in front of the camera, thereby insulating the White males who continue to dominate the executive suites from having to share their power to make industry-defining decisions. . . . There is little evidence that the structures that form the industry's creative ecosystem (e.g., the executive suites, production units, marketing units, talent agencies, or writers' rooms) have been reshaped in any meaningful way.[43]

The same conditions obtain in many other places. Although there is no denying increased diversity as well as the existence and success of shows that don't cater directly to white audiences, whiteness continues to frame who gets to tell what stories, who they should try to appeal to, and whose perspective to exclude.

White's Entertainment

One thing that unites the three forms of popular culture above is that they are mostly white phenomena; they are particular rather than universal in the sense that they are written, produced, directed, cast, illustrated, or otherwise created largely by people who can be racialized as white under the present racial formations. And they are generally designed to appeal to audiences that are conceived as white. Yet they are not labeled as particular and racialized in the way they are in the headings above, as "white movies," "white shows," "white books," and so on. White popular culture is the norm, the universal standard, and anything that is not white must be labeled as such (this goes far beyond popular entertainments; Bonilla-Silva writes about how HBCUs [historically black colleges and universities] has no HWCUs corollary, for instance).

The racial grammar of popular whiteness extends beyond the examples discussed in this chapter. In these and other forms of entertainment, white people are the majority and norm; people of color are rare, and usually play minor or stereotypical roles. Many story lines reinforce racial boundaries, uphold the status quo, or present a rosy view of racial affairs. Illustrations of the latter can be seen in cross-racial "buddy movies" or "white savior" narratives. Buddy movies are a financial windfall for studios and provide a feel-good boost to viewers: "Whites want to feel good about themselves by imagining they can have friends across the racial divide. But those imaginary friends are depicted in a one-sided, stereotypical, and ultimately accommodating fashion."[44] White savior narratives amplify or invent efforts by white people to help people of color suffering adversity in order to center white people in narratives that aren't about them. This happens even when the stories are based on the historical experiences of people of color, and it promotes an image of individual white moral fortitude as the solution to racism. These movies offer diffuse messages of unity and compassion, reduce complicated systemic problems to easy solutions, make distinctions between "good" and "bad" white people who can choose—contra Charles W. Mills's racial contract—to be racist or not, and thus allow white viewers to both scapegoat "real" racists and feel better about themselves for identifying with a white person who shows compassion to the oppressed. The list could go on.

Our entertainments are not innocent or neutral; they are deeply political racial projects that shape and frame the world.

Children's literature, superheroes, sitcoms, and our other entertainments are sites for the production and dissemination of knowledge. As such, they are not innocent or neutral; they are deeply political racial projects that shape and frame the world as it is understood by white people and people of color alike. Increasingly, that framing obscures far more than it explains.

DON'T CALL ME WHITE!

Perhaps somewhat optimistically, George M. Fredrickson wrote that "the defeat of Nazi Germany, the desegregation of the American South in the 1960s, and the establishment of majority rule in South Africa suggests that regimes based on biological racism and its cultural essentialist equivalent are a thing of the past." But, he added, "racism does not require the full and explicit support of the state and the law," and most important in this context, institutional and individual discrimination against people considered racially different can both persist and flourish under the "illusion of nonracism."[1] A look at the current state of "racial" affairs around the world would suggest that such patterns are persistent indeed. To that end, this chapter discusses so-called color blindness, and outlines its emergence in Sweden and the United States as primary examples. After that, the related concept of "color-blind racism" and the increasingly common talk of "reverse racism" are explored, followed by some recent instances of how color-blind racism and reverse racism accusations have been mobilized in order to protect as well as obscure white supremacy in several majority-white countries.

Color Blindness, Hegemon of Our Age

It is a widely accepted commonplace among white-racialized people that racism, with a few exceptions, is a thing of the past. Racism in this view is usually equated with the explicit hatred of specific groups of people. There is, in Robin DiAngelo's terms, a "good/bad binary" in place in the United States. The racist ideal type is viewed as ignorant, bigoted, prejudiced, mean-spirited, old, southern people; the nonracist ideal type is progressive, educated, open-minded, well-intentioned, young, and northern.[2] Adjusting the geographic stereotypes, the same list can readily be applied to Sweden as well. Racism in Sweden has long been equated with Nazism and apartheid, and the view of racism as a clear, derogatory racial ideology still holds true for many, even in public and governmental contexts. One report noted that representatives of Swedish institutions—politicians and civil servants, union reps, and researchers—even seemed to find it difficult to utter words like "racism" and "discrimination" in relation to fellow people in power or about themselves.[3] The good/bad distinction is part of many Swedes' self-image: antiracism is widely considered a part of the national identity, and "the 'good' antiracist Swedishness enables distancing from the readily identifiable 'bad' white racists in the shape of the Sweden Democrats."[4]

Because of the dominance of the interpersonal and ideological framing of racism as something "bad people" do, the suggestion that someone's speech or actions have racist effects is frequently interpreted as a moral accusation. Indeed, linguist Teun A. van Dijk writes, accusations of racism among white-racialized people tend

> to be seen as more serious than racist attitudes or actions themselves, e.g., because they disrupt ingroup solidarity and smooth ingroup encounters: they are felt to ruin the "good atmosphere" of interactions and situations. Moreover, such accusations are seen to impose taboos, prevent free speech and a "true" or "honest" assessment of the ethnic situation. In other words, denials of racism often turn into counter-accusations of intolerant and intolerable anti-racism.[5]

Or it should be added, of reverse racism when the speaker is not themselves racialized as part of the white "us."

It is a widely accepted commonplace among white-racialized people that racism, with a few exceptions, is a thing of the past.

Michael Omi and Howard Winant, along with many others, suggest that the dominant racial formation of the current historical moment is that of color blindness. Color blindness rests on the idea that "racial thinking" is no longer a salient influence on people's perceptions and attitudes, and no longer influences individuals, collectives, or institutions' practices. From this understanding, it is easy to conclude or accept the claim that now that racial legal segregation is no longer in effect and explicit, inter-personal racism is generally considered a bad thing, white and nonwhite people are playing on a level field. "Indeed," write Omi and Winant, "it is said that the most effective anti-racist consciousness, policy, and practice is simply to ignore race."[6]

Not everybody accepts the color-blind view, and there is much difference among those who do both in how they understand and act according to it, but it nevertheless has had a strong social, cultural, institutional, and political impact in many countries. Color blindness is perhaps particularly strong in the contemporary United States and Sweden, albeit in somewhat different ways and arrived at through different routes. Color blindness in the United States took its current shape after the civil rights era. It is rooted in the claim that the goals of the movement have been achieved, and as a result, and because legalized and explicit racial discrimination has been abolished, the United States has transitioned into a "postracial" society.

In Sweden, the historical trajectory of color blindness begins in the 1950s with some first, hesitant steps away from the earlier widespread acceptance of racial ideology that broke into a full run by the late 1960s. Slowly, through grassroots politics as well as domestic and foreign policy alike, Sweden emerged as a loud anti-imperial, anticolonial, and antiracist voice on the international stage, and walked the associated walk through substantial foreign aid along with clear support for anticolonial and civil rights movements around the world. Swedish leaders, activists, and intellectuals worked to position the country as a radical supporter of social justice, equality, and human rights. "Almost overnight," write sociologist Catrin Lundström and colleague Tobias Hübinette, Sweden "transformed from a nation that had been almost completely obsessed with race to the world's most anti-racist and colorblind country."[7]

On the national arena, this transformation was accomplished through large-scale adoptions of nonwhite children coupled with the West's proportionately largest reception of immigrants, multicultural and equality legislation, and an accompanying denial that racial discrimination happened in Sweden.[8] Through these efforts, Sweden could project an image of anticolonial and postcolonial whiteness—a sort of moral white supremacy. While the 1990s had seen a resurgence of neo-Nazi and racist groups as well as racially motivated murders, and a racially focused serial killer, the word "race" was more or less expunged from the political lexicon and public discourse around the turn of the millennium. Today, for good and considerable ill, Swedes barely speak about race at all.

The past two decades have seen the continued spread and, because of changed law enforcement priorities after 9/11, largely unchecked growth of racist extremism, Islamophobia, and antimulticultural sentiment. At the same time, Sweden's demographics have continued to change, and neoliberal economics and politics have hollowed out the welfare state, leaving nonwhite populations most exposed. Currently, Sweden remains one of few officially antiracist countries in the world, but it nonetheless stands without an official language to put that stance into practice. It is therefore not surprising that it is also one of the most segregated countries in the "developed" world.

Sociologists Charles Gallagher and France Winddance Twine offer a diagnosis of color blindness that applies equally well to the United States, about which they write, as it does to Sweden: "The concept of race (and racism) has been reconstituted, repackaged, and offered up in the media as an easily digested dichotomy; on one hand society's presentation of self is one of colourblindness and on the other a minority of the population continues to embrace outdated racist ideologies."[9]

As the preceding pages have argued, color blindness does not seem as successful as its proponents claim. Instead of producing more equality, color blindness might be allowing white people to disavow explicit racial hatred without considering systemic racism, leaving existing inequalities to fester and grow. Or as Ibram X. Kendi puts it, color blindness is "akin to the notion of being 'not racist'—as with the 'not racist,' the colorblind individual, by ostensibly failing to see race, fails to see racism and falls into [structural] racist passivity."[10] A well-known example from the present would be countering the claim that "Black Lives Matter" with the assertion that "All Lives Matter": by universalizing, the speaker denies the importance of racial formation in creating a situation in which, in the United States and many other places, Black lives currently seem not to matter, at least not nearly as much as white lives do.

Color-blind and Reverse Racism

If race is no longer a relevant factor in social and cultural life, if it is not a determining factor in economics and politics, how can we account for continuing inequality and discrimination? According to Eduardo Bonilla-Silva, there has developed a whole host of explanations and rationalizations for why people racialized as white carry no responsibility for the status of people of color, such as "certain people" don't work hard enough, don't have the right values or ideals, or belong to a culture that doesn't foster productive lifestyles. He labels the source of these kinds of explanations as an ideology of "color-blind racism," which "explains racial inequalities as the outcome of nonracial dynamics."[11]

Color-blind racism centers on the assertion that racism is no longer a problem; difficulties and challenges occur on an individual basis, rather than on collective or institutional ones. In Bonilla-Silva's definition, color-blind racism works through four central frames:

- *abstract liberalism*, which involves using ideas associated with political and economic liberalism, such as equal opportunity, individual merit, or individual choice, to explain away or ignore structural or systemic racial inequalities

- *naturalization*, which rests on suggesting that racialized phenomena are natural, arguing, for example, that segregation is natural because "like attracts like" rather than a product of racial formation and socioeconomic organization

- *cultural racism*, which foregrounds cultural explanations for the social standing of minorities

- *minimization of racism*, which suggests that discrimination is no longer a central factor in many minorities' life chances—a stance that with only minimal caricaturing, can be summarized in the idea that "race doesn't matter anymore and racism is over, so get over the past already."[12]

If color blindness can be understood as a denial that race remains a social, cultural, economic, and political factor in the supposedly postracial world, color-blind racism can be understood as speech, behaviors, and rationalizations that treat racist outcomes as grounded in something other than racial formation. Correctly acknowledging that race is not a biological fact and thus refusing to speak about race at all doesn't mean racism will just go away on its own, however. Race remains a social fact because not everyone views it as a social construct. It is therefore essential to be aware of the effects racial formation continues to have. As Omi and Winant note, color blindness has gone from a call for racial equality and inclusion to now being "largely an ideological framework for effacing race consciousness."[13] As such, as opposed to counteracting racism, color blindness makes it harder to name and challenge it—as seen in the example of Sweden above.

It has also created new paths for racism and white supremacy. In a world where race supposedly has no meaning, talk about race becomes suspect. Hence it is often assumed that only people of color have a stake in talking about racism and so are responsible for any "race problems" that may exist—*they* are the ones who play the "race card"; *they* demand "preferential treatment"; *they* use racism as

Correctly acknowledging that race is not a biological fact and thus refusing to speak about race at all doesn't mean racism will just go away on its own.

a "shield from criticism." This type of backlash is a typical illustration of color-blind racism. Another common feature of color blindness and color-blind racism is the trope of so-called reverse racism. In the United States, this idea started to gain footing shortly after the civil rights legislation of the mid-1960s. Code words that circumscribed race while serving the purpose of racial reaction and white supremacist ideology replaced much of the explicit racist language that had been common earlier, but they were less effective in achieving the desired goals. More was needed to oppose the racial reforms underway in affirmative action, fair housing and fair lending policies, and the like.

The Nixon campaign's "Southern Strategy" had successfully used coded language to dog whistle white supremacy to enough voters that it won Richard Nixon the White House in 1968. From that beginning, opposition to "reverse discrimination" could be "mainstreamed." Antiracist activists were becoming increasingly aware of how inadequate the post–civil rights reforms had been, but by the 1970s, neoconservatives began using a group rights–based logic to direct those reforms toward white supremacist ends. The implementation of civil rights policy was recast and reformulated as an attack on white people, taking away resources they deserved and redistributing them to people of color, who in a steady parade of public and academic discourse have been accused of one cultural deficiency after another.

As Omi and Winant summarize it, "The use of civil rights logic to protect whites from anti-racist reforms—the 'reverse racism' argument as legal, academic, and above all political ideology—was a more effective *rearticulation* of the 'post-civil rights' era than the new right's 'code words' had been."[14] A number of landmark cases affirmed this shift, "subvert[ing] equality by vesting the expectations of whites that what is unequal in fact will be regarded as equal in law."[15] Reverse racism has since been taken over by many other people, in many places. It's been getting more common in Sweden in recent years. The nationalist political Right now frequently speaks about reverse racism as a matter of course, often in terms of *svenskfientlighet* (hostility to Swedes). Reverse racism is more commonly used in media discussions while svenskfientlighet is more commonly seen on social media and in the so-called alternative media sphere of the extreme and alt-right. Bridging the divide between the margin and center, the Sweden Democrats proposed a motion in Parliament in 2013 to "intensify work against svenskfientlighet" and invited all parliamentary parties to join a "network against svenskfientlighet" in 2020. Adding insult to injury, the invitation was sent on November 9, the anniversary of the Nazi *Kristallnacht* pogrom. Svenskfientlighet has been a party issue since at least 2008.[16]

Color blindness and reverse racism are also tied to the aggrieved entitlement of angry white men and others.

Affirmative action policies, antidiscrimination initiatives, and other attempts to redress historically rooted inequalities are viewed by many white people as forms of reverse discrimination. Jobs, benefits, and advancements they consider "theirs" are instead going to "undeserving" Others simply because they are not white. Examples of historical discrimination against other groups are used to argue against any specific legacies or structural disadvantages stemming from, for instance, slavery. A common rhetorical trope in the United States is the contention that racial redress is a hindrance to nonwhite integration and progress. The villain is often "the liberal establishment, whose misguided policies . . . have retarded [sic] the natural assimilative processes by which yesterday's immigrants were eventually made over."[17] One writer even claims that the founding fathers' vision was of a nation for all, without restrictions on immigration. Matthew Frye Jacobson dryly notes that some might regard the "free white persons" naturalization clause, in effect from 1790 to 1952, as a restriction. The same author suggests that European groups took between 80 and 120 years to fully integrate. In this vein, he claims that Black US Americans' "mass migration" began only around 60 years prior to his writing (2001), ignoring that most African American's didn't "migrate," and that four centuries of oppressive racial formation have created a US economy, culture, and society that is actively stacked against Black US Americans.

Narratives like this, that deny the salience of whiteness in integration and assimilation histories, must deny not only the presence on what is now US American soil of Black people since the 1600s but also the presence of Latinx peoples in several US states before they were incorporated into the United States and the histories of Native American people that long predate the presence of white settlers. Such color-blind rewriting of US American history is not only antihistorical but hinges on the denial of centuries of racialized violence, marginalization, oppression, and exploitation too. This type of narrative is common. It has been taught in US schools for years and was briefly touted by the Trump administration in its final days. The 1776 Commission that authored an ahistorical report based on this type of historiography grew out of an executive order signed by Donald J. Trump rooted in color blindness and reverse racism accusations, and it was not the only attempt to paper over growing global critiques of racism in fall 2020. What follows are a few examples out of many possible ones, intended to illustrate how color-blind rhetoric along with claims about reverse racism have been mobilized in different political, public, and popular cultural contexts to argue against engagement with racist history or oppressive racial formations. Though taken from different contexts, and though they do so in different ways, they all buttress white hegemony.

Reverse Racism Revolts

The earlier chapter on white words ended by noting that having words to name whiteness and the effects of white racial formation is likely not going to end its hegemony any time soon. But it would seem that at the very least, the widespread and growing dissemination of critical race theory (CRT) and critical whiteness studies' vocabularies are making some elites nervous. At least three major racial projects couched in terms of color blindness and reverse racism were launched in late 2020 in the United States, United Kingdom, and France.

On September 22, 2020, President Trump signed an executive order on "Combating Race and Sex Stereotyping." The order aimed to prohibit federal employees, contractors, and grant recipients from engaging with what the order calls "critical race theory"—CRT is painted with a broad brush largely divorced from actual work in the area, and many of its critics are hard-pressed to define what they mean by CRT when asked—and concepts like white privilege, and discouraged diversity education and training. It bemoaned that today, "many people are pushing a different vision of America that is grounded in hierarchies based on collective social and political identities rather than in the inherent and equal dignity of every person as an individual," and are resurrecting rhetoric from nineteenth-century slavery apologists. Phrased differently, the executive order misrepresented CRT and critiques of whiteness, among other things, in order to call antiracism the "real" racism. While the Biden administration overturned it in late January 2021, the order had already led some colleges and universities to suspend diversity training as well as cancel events for fear of losing funding. The order gave rhetorics of reverse racism, white dispossession, and white denial the imprimatur of the nation's highest office and turned them into managing principles of the federal government. Many others have followed suit in state legislatures.

Then, on October 20, 2020, during a debate about a UK Black History Month in Parliament, conservative members of Parliament turned the spotlight on CRT. The school of thought, one member argued, was "a barrier to this being a country based on 'merit and character.'"[18] Another said that rather than structures of race and class, "where you live, the job you do and the type of housing you in live in explains the increased risk to ethnic minority groups." As has been noted above, these are all racialized aspects of social and economic life. Through their choice of examples, and perhaps somewhat ironically, the conservative member of Parliament thus framed their opposition to CRT as an almost textbook case of Bonilla-Silva's abstract liberalism and in so doing almost naturalized the chosen racialized structures out of existence.

Finally, on November 2, 2020, a group of a hundred French academics published an open letter in agreement with France's minister of education that antiracist scholarship had been responsible for "conditioning" the murderer of schoolteacher Samuel Paty on October 16: "Indigenist, racialist and 'decolonial' ideologies (imported from North American campuses) are very present there [in French universities], fueling a hatred of 'whites' and of France," wrote the academics.[19] The legacies of French colonialism and imperialism, and the country's growing Islamophobia, were all downplayed in favor of forceful claims about reverse racism.

Aside from centering on reverse racism, these three projects are also united in their color-blind roots. Although addressing different societies, they all attempt to prevent discussions of race and racism from taking place in universities and government institutions, and if possible, in public. In arguing against continued investigations of whiteness, the texts all mobilize color blindness to erect limits to acceptable speech while limiting critical discourse about power and white supremacy. Since these high-profile attempts to condemn CRT, many more editorials, policy proposals, and legislative bids have been launched to curtail critical scrutiny and discussion of whiteness wherever it may appear, particularly in the United States. The only people who stand to benefit from such comprehensive denials of the past, present, and future impact of race and whiteness are white people, or those aspiring to white racialization. While these reverse racism revolts were presented as serving the well-being of politics and education, they were at heart a form of backlash rooted in white rage. Around the same time, another form of backlash mobilized white fragility in the defense of culture.

Jan Guillou's "Racial Mystique"

Guillou, a well-respected Swedish author and leftist pundit, has a direct line to Swedish opinion pages. In October 2020, he used his access to vent about an interview with Kayo Mpoyi and Judith Kiros, two Black women authors in Sweden, about the struggles and pitfalls of trying to succeed as a racialized writer in a country that is widely viewed as homogeneously white.[20] The conversation offended him because to read it was to be racialized as a "white man" and by implication, according to Guillou himself, a "less desirable reader."[21]

Guillou dutifully acknowledged that he, as a white man, isn't "an ideal" critic of "young Afro-Swedish as well as female literary debutantes." But since nobody else seemed to be either, he chose to take up the mantle. He found it both "telling" and "disturbing" that the conversation had passed unremarked. To him, it contained "odd thoughts" about the importance of skin color—something he repeatedly classifies as a "racial mystique." To Guillou, his (imagined) interlocutors—whom he repeatedly, insistently calls "colleague," as if to force them into the mold he prefers—are Swedish and, in his presentation, that is all they are. On the other hand, they seem in Guillou's mind to think there's something special in their skin that produces different writing and reading abilities in people.

While Guillou deplores his subjects' imagined racial mystique, he engages in an "authorial mystique" that highlights how color blindness can lead to historical distortions. As an author, Guillou writes, you "direct yourself at readers' thought and emotional worlds, not their skin color." So when Mpoyi and Kiros mention adapting their work to a white audience, he cannot contain his bafflement: How would an author do that? He then asks, rhetorically, and from either earnest or willful ignorance, "In what ways did James Baldwin and Toni Morrison [*sic*] adapt" their work to a white or Black audience?

This is a good question, if asked sincerely, but Guillou's implication seems to be that they didn't "adapt" their work—that is, have an authorial address—but rather were simply "authors." Morrison, however, famously and repeatedly stated that she wrote for Black people, refused to conform to a "white gaze," and embraced the label "Black writer." Furthermore, Morrison had explicitly noted that "for both black and white American writers, there is no escape from racially inflected language, and the work writers do to unhobble the imagination from the demands of that language is complicated, interesting, and definitive." Claiming that literature is "universal" and "race-free," she remarked, risks "lobotomizing" that literature.[22] Baldwin often explicitly and directly interpolated his audience as Black or white. His already-cited piece about white guilt repeatedly implores white readers to hear him, and in his 1962 "Letter from a Region in My Mind," he wrote, among other things, "Whatever white people do not know about Negroes reveals, precisely and inexorably, what they do not know about themselves."[23] Morrison and Baldwin, then, didn't only "adapt" their work to one audience or another. They wrote from a clear understanding of the racial formation under which they lived, and which they knew they couldn't escape or deny.

Omitting that Sweden has its own racial formation, as powerfully suggested by his continued recourse to US American examples, Guillou ultimately takes on the task of adjudicating what is or isn't permitted for Black people to feel. Immediately after his question about Baldwin and Morrison, he writes, "The vagueness that pervades this type of neoracist line of thought seems to be coming out of the *legitimate rage* that exists within the Black Lives Matter revolt, as if some kind of counterracism could be excused in the heat of battle."

Despite adopting a color-blind position, Guillou clearly has no difficulty in racializing Black people, in Sweden or abroad. Nor does he shy away from racializing himself and taking the stance of a white victim. But when the idea that racialization can lead to different experiences for different people is broached, it turns into racial mystique and "mumbo jumbo" that Guillou compares to other mumbo jumbo that "in its day," curtailed Black people's right to vote in the United States. This claim doesn't account for the fact that attempted and actual voter suppression had disproportionately affected Black people and people of color, and had been a topic of discussion surrounding the then-imminent 2020 US presidential election. Nor does it account for the evidence that anti-Black racism is thriving in Sweden.

Guillou's admission of not being the "ideal critic" of young Black women turns out to be truer than he probably intended. The text is permeated by white habitus and epistemic ignorance of racial formation and racism in Sweden and the United States, in the past and present. Thus the text works to reassert color blindness, aggressively and through white fragility, via accusations of reverse racism, minimizations of race, and the individualized, patronizing, and paternalistic suggestion that letting Mpoyi and Kiros speak about their experiences—or "mean that Black people have a different right to express themselves in racist ways," as Guillou puts it—is to be racist oneself by treating them "like the less knowledgeable or children who don't fully know what they're saying." Letting Black people be racist, he concludes, should be impossible for anyone who respects democracy. By implication, and by questioning their commitment to equality and democracy,

Guillou is implying that Mpoyi and Kiros aren't as Swedish as he'd earlier indicated. Guillou is generally known as a left-leaning person, but being opposed to some forms of power doesn't necessarily mean that one cannot exert other forms of power over those with less privilege.

"Don't Call Me White"

California-based punk band NOFX has long courted controversy through its public statements and lyrics. Many songs address ethnoracial, gender, or sexual identity, often flippantly. The song "Kill All the White Man" (1992) can be read as a critique of colonialism, but is performed in "aural blackface" with singer Fat Mike affecting a "Jamaican" accent and "broken" English. Whether the song critiques colonialism or its discontents is a matter of debate among fans and critics. Some see it as a sarcastic jab against anticolonial struggles, and others as "white genocide" advocacy. The prerogative of white men to make light of colonial exploitation is rarely questioned, however.

Many other NOFX songs have been similarly subject to scrutiny, but the band's most famous engagement with whiteness has attracted little critical attention. Its 1994 song "Don't Call Me White" disavows whiteness completely. While older than the examples above, it is worth looking closer at precisely because it has retained a "cult" position in a subculture filled with self-identifying antiracists. The first verse acknowledges that "language breeds stereotype" but wonders "what's the explanation for the malice, for the spite" perceived to be associated with the word "white." The second verse claims difference from slavery-linked nonwhiteness and possibly highlights Fat Mike's Jewish American heritage, in the lines "I wasn't brought here, I was born/Circumcised, categorized, allegiance sworn." This feeds into a rejection of white racialization ("Does this mean I have to take such shit/For being fair skinned? No!"), which is opposed with individualism ("I ain't part of no conspiracy, I'm just your average Joe"). The third verse links whiteness to conformity and ordinariness ("A buttoned collar, starched and bleached / Constricting veins, the blood flow to the brain slows / They're so fuckin ordinary white"), and rejects both, while the bridge repeats the disavowal of racial self-identification in favor of individualism ("go ahead and label me an asshole 'cause I can / Accept responsibility, for what I've done, but not for who I am").[24]

As such, the song reads like a racial project based in white fragility. It emphatically frames a defensive position in response to being perceived in racial terms as white, and disavows racialization in favor of individualism. If the first verse's reference to circumcisions is meant to signify Jewishness, it also seems likely the song takes recourse to Frye Jacobson's "Ellis Island whiteness" to deny white privilege.[25] It's impossible to overstate the ongoing history of US American anti-Semitism, but neither can one deny that white-passing Jewish Americans have historically been closer to whiteness than Black people or people of color.[26] Further, Fat Mike has noted that the song is explicitly about debates about how to address the legacy of slavery: "a lot of people may say it's not PC, but it's stuff I was doing in debate class in college, and we were debating whether African Americans should get reparations for slavery. That's what that song's about."[27] In this context, the second verse's reference to slavery reads as an example of the "minimization of race" by seemingly pushing Black oppression back into the mists of history, sidestepping the racial realities of the song's mid-1990s' United States.

Combined, the lyrics express a common white avoidance strategy, as if saying, "I'm not white, I'm an individual. And besides, my family history doesn't include slavery so I have no stake in white supremacy." Ongoing white privileges and the deep-rooted racist structures that secure them are discounted offhand, as if their benefits are optional. "The disavowal of responsibility for slavery," writes George Lipsitz,

> never acknowledges how the existence of slavery
> and the exploitation of Black labor after
> emancipation created opportunities that penalized
> *all* Blacks and benefited *all* whites even those who
> did not own slaves and even those whose families
> emigrated to the United States after slavery ended.

Rather, it seems to hold that because not all white people owned slaves, no white people can be held accountable or inconvenienced by the legacy of slavery.[28]

"Don't Call Me White," now considered a "classic" by many white punk fans, therefore dresses something reactionary in rebellious garb. While claiming to disavow whiteness, the song fits into a larger pattern: it employs white fragility to counter the threat of being racialized as white, which is positioned as a form of reverse racism. For people of color, and many who can't pass as straight, white men, the white-dominated punk scene can be far less welcoming. Poet and cultural critic Hanif Abdurraqib summarizes a central tension:

In the punk landscape, we are often given imagery that reflects the most real truths of this scene: the exclusion of people of color, of women, of the queer community, and that exclusion being sometimes explicit, sometimes violent, but almost always in direct conflict with the idea of punk rock as a place for rebellion against (among other things) identity.[29]

Punk's overall image is system critical, but songs like "Don't Call Me White" (or Minor Threat's "Guilty of Being White" or Blood for Blood's "White Trash Anthem") show

how closely it can hew to structures of dominance and oppression. They offer a comforting thought that keeps white supremacist racial formation in place: the idea that you can be neither signatory nor beneficiary of the racial contract.

Color Blindness and Reverse Racism: Scaffolding for White Supremacy

It is difficult to say which came first, color blindness or reverse racism. According to Omi and Winant, the emergence of reverse racism contained the seeds of so-called color-blind ideology. The claim that such a thing as reverse racism exists is rooted in the idea that those who speak about it are themselves "race neutral" and antiracist: "To understand the 'true meaning' of civil rights," Omi and Winant write about the emergence of the reverse racism discourse in the US American context, "was to declare that race would henceforth be 'irrelevant' to the distribution of scarce resources like jobs or college admissions."[30] But color blindness goes a step beyond reverse racism. Color blindness doesn't merely claim to be neutral on issues of race but rather to do to away with race entirely—a notion exemplified with particular clarity in assertions that the United States is a postracial society after the election of Obama in 2008, or in Sweden, where race has been gradually expunged from the official lexicon since around the turn of the twentieth century.

While this racial project is based on the established and (for most) undeniable fact that race is not a biological fact, it fails to reckon with the continued existence of race as a social fact. Too often, advocates of color blindness speak of racism while denying race or racialization, creating a chimera of a "racism without racists," to borrow Bonilla-Silva's phrase. This can cause serious problems. As Gallagher and Twine noted in 2017, "The perception by a majority of whites that we are now colourblind is why the Black Lives Matter movement was so jarring for some whites; in a colourblind America 'all lives' should matter and to privilege black lives over others is, from a colorblind perspective a form of racism."[31] In a world where race isn't supposed to matter, pointing out that it nevertheless still does is a serious heresy.

Today, a color-blind view tends to offer a clear division between the world as it was, before race was revealed as a lie, and the world after. Since the idea of racial essentialism has been largely discredited, we shouldn't dwell on the past. But the past doesn't cease to have happened simply because most white people today understand things differently than our ancestors. And it doesn't cease to effect the present, to have a real, concrete legacy. Cultures that have been destroyed and peoples who have been murdered by European conquests won't simply reappear; extracted

In a world where race isn't supposed to matter, pointing out that it nevertheless still does is a serious heresy.

wealth won't return to former colonies and remuneration won't simply be paid out, retroactively, to the descendants of enslaved people. Intergenerational wealth won't just appear in the bank accounts of those who have been structurally prevented from accumulating it. Native American, Aboriginal and Torres Strait Island, and Sámi peoples, or countless others who have been disposed and relocated, can't just reclaim their ancestral lands.

Rather than face up to these and too many other injustices to mention, many white people around the world hide behind color blindness and reverse racism accusations to simultaneously disavow the continuing reality of racial formation, racism, and white supremacy, deny people of color their own experiences, and sometimes take them over for oneself. Color blindness frequently fosters or presupposes an epistemology of white ignorance in the form of a simultaneous denial of the continued salience of race and an inability or unwillingness to acknowledge how, despite being discredited, race continues to taint much of contemporary life. Crucially, however, as Omi and Winant note, to "challenge colorblindness you must be race-conscious. But to police the ideological boundaries of colorblindness you must *also* be race-conscious."[32] Remember Guillou, whose argument hinges on racializing Mpoyi and Kiros so he can chastise them for not being color-blind like himself. This pushback against those who speak about racism is a core feature of color-blind racism.

Color blindness and reverse racism can thus be viewed as forms of "scaffolding" for white supremacy in our own time; claims that race doesn't matter and that those who dare speak of racialization are the "real racists" serve extremely well to keep racialized injustices and inequalities firmly in place. With that, the book has come full circle: even in a color-blind world, where race isn't supposed to matter, whiteness functions as a system of social control.

WHITHER WHITENESS?

In the final round of the 2021 Eurovision Song Contest, the host country, the Netherlands, was represented by Suriname-born Jeangu Macrooy with the song "Birth of a New Age." The song opens with a line about "skin as rich as the starlit night," contains imagery about echoing the names of "heroes burned at the stake" and being the "rage that melts the chains," and the song returns time and again to affirm "your rhythm is rebellion." The chorus, repeating "yu no man broko mi" (you cannot break me) over and over, and cycling in the lyric "mi na afu sensi" (I'm half a cent) at regular intervals, is sung in Sranan Tongo, a Surinamese Dutch- and English-based creole language with origins in the country's years as a colony of England (1650–1667) and the Netherlands (1667–1954). While Macrooy emphasizes that it also speaks to queer empowerment and the COVID-19 pandemic, it is difficult not to see the song as also a discussion of colonial repression and Black empowerment.[1] The imagery and choreography of the performance heightened the impression that the song celebrated Blackness and perseverance in the face of racialized oppression. Hearing the words and seeing the moves performed by Black representatives of the Netherlands, a country that often claims "white innocence" while being marked by widespread racism, makes them all the more notable.[2]

In the comments to the official music video for the song on YouTube or articles about it, some celebrate Macrooy and stress the importance of seeing Dutch history in a critical way, while others follow established white supremacist or color-blind racist patterns. To some, Macrooy, a Black man singing parts of the song in Sranan Tongo, doesn't represent the Netherlands. In these comments, citizenship is defined as it commonly is in the United States, Sweden, the United Kingdom, or France, for example: through whiteness. To others, the song's politics are a source of anger or disgust; some frame the song as "universal"—"a struggle for all people in life"—in order to make it easier to listen to because in the words of one commenter, "If I see it as a blm song, I t[h]row my telephone out of the window." A final type of comment that permeates the response holds that we need to stop dwelling on the past.

While the Macrooy song is powerful, it wasn't chosen here because it is unique. To the contrary, it was picked because it was the most recent public example of some common phenomena when this conclusion was first drafted. Sweden's representative in the contest, Tousin "Tusse" Chiza, was similarly met with racist comments because he doesn't meet the vision many hold of what a Swede should look like. The preceding chapters have presented several illustrations of the so-called color-blind resistance to any public discussion of race or racism, and calls to refocus such conversations from specific experiences to supposed universals. For that reason, it is more fruitful here to look at one of the major points of contention arising around the song and in many other recent talk about whiteness: how to view the past.

Color blindness as a racial formation is largely present oriented. The color-blind gaze often focuses on the now, but it is intimately tied up with the past. Two contradictory ways of relating to the past seem to dominate the discourse. On the one hand, as already suggested above, there are many who argue that what is past is past, and the present is qualitatively different. There are many reasons for taking this stance. As James Baldwin framed it in 1965, when writing about many white US Americans, they may be "dimly, or vividly, aware that the history they have fed themselves is mainly a lie, but they do not know how to release themselves from it."[3] Or as literary critic and essayist Sven Lindqvist noted forty years later about many white Australians' discomfort with the growing interest in Australian race relations,

Color blindness as a racial formation is largely present oriented.

They used to see themselves as law-abiding settlers, who had brought the blessings of civilization to the indigenous inhabitants of Australia. They are understandably reluctant to let historical research rob them of this beautiful picture and substitute a history of mass killing, land theft, rape, kidnapping, and other outrages. Many prefer to turn a blind eye to the growing mountain of evidence of their forefathers' violence and racism.[4]

Both perspectives perhaps suggest a measure of good faith in the suppression of history or an inability to acknowledge past atrocities. As Lindqvist observed elsewhere, bad faith approaches exist too. "It is not knowledge that is lacking," he wrote in *Exterminate All the Brutes* (1992). "The educated general public has always largely known that outrages have been committed and are being committed in the name of Progress, Civilization, Socialism, Democracy, and the Market. At all times it has also been profitable to deny or suppress such knowledge."[5] A major problem with the past-is-past perspective, no matter the reason it's adopted, is that the past isn't, in fact, past; it is insistently, irreducibly present. Colonialism, chattel slavery, imperialism, and segregation—many of which are still practiced in new guises—have legacies that deeply affect people all over the world. Silence and denial have serious consequences.

Another common strategy is not to deny the relevance of the past to the present but rather to directly oppose any attempt to nuance or critique established historical narratives. Whenever beloved children's books are scrutinized for racist imagery that was more acceptable to white people in their own time and their suitability for continued reading is questioned, the cry quickly rings out that critics are attempting to "erase history." When symbols celebrating Confederate figures, the majority of which were erected long after the Civil War as "markers to an *idealized* version of *white* southern history" during periods of rising white supremacy, are criticized, the same accusation arises.[6] It happened again in summer 2020, in the United States, United Kingdom, and beyond, when statues and other commemorative markers of slaveholders, colonists, and white supremacists were torn down or destroyed. The Trump administration's 1776 Commission published a report meant to promote "patriotic education" that served as an officially sanctioned attempt to quiet critical debates about race in US American history and was presented as "a dispositive rebuttal of reckless 're-education' attempts that seek to reframe American history around the idea that the United States is not an exceptional country but an evil one."[7] Here they echoed, for example, Keith Windschuttle, whose *Fabrication of Aboriginal History, Volume One* (2002) argued that "no genocide was committed, the massacres [of Aboriginal peoples] were legitimate police actions, and there was no reign of terror based on widespread violence. . . . It is all a gigantic forgery, intended to deprive [white] Australians of the right to be proud of their history."[8] While charges of erasing or altering history are levied at many people or groups, for many different reasons, they nearly always share the same core contradiction: the claimed purpose may be to defend history, but the goal is to reinstate or manufacture a collective memory that serves to protect white supremacist narratives and power.

Macrooy's song, on the other hand, invites a critical engagement with the past in a popularized form. As such, it can be situated in relation to a major contemporary current in many fields, united by the drive to engage the past on critical terms, face up to the atrocities committed in the name of colonialism, and decenter the whiteness that has been central to grand Eurocentric narratives for centuries. To borrow Lindqvist's words, "As historical memory is gradually democratized and globalized, we [white people] have to get used to being seen not just as pioneers and benefactors but also as perpetrators of outrages, sometimes of continent-wide crimes."[9] As the examples above show, many white people are deeply resistant to occupying the role of white person, with all the historical baggage it implies. That only makes it even more urgent to keep pushing in that direction.

One of the central drives in critical whiteness studies, repeated in many studies and overviews of the research area, is the continuing need to "make whiteness strange," as Richard Dyer once phrased it, to make it always visible. The impulse behind his book *White* was "to come to see that position of white authority in order to help undermine it."[10] Peggy McIntosh wrote that "to redesign social systems, we need first to acknowledge their colossal unseen dimensions."[11] Tying into color blindness discourses, Steve Garner notes that "the systemic exertion of power and reaping of benefits can be sustained only if whiteness requires its practitioners *not to see* the benefits accruing them from structural advantages, but as manifestations of individual failings."[12] And Charles Gallagher and France Winndance Twine, trying to identify what is common in the otherwise disparate area of whiteness studies, maintain that "at its core the focus on whiteness, has always been to make visible those institutions, social and cultural practices that redistribute resources along racial lines. The goal is to reveal the power inherent in whiteness."[13]

On that measure, whiteness studies has been a success in some ways: a critical perspective on whiteness is now present in many contexts, as a way of making whiteness visible, and it has become more common to see critical discussion of whiteness in public forums and on social media where there had previously been little. This drive further builds on a history that long predates the foundation of academic whiteness studies; the literature of "white estrangement" has been attempting "the important critical project of unveiling Whiteness *to itself* by providing a revealing counternarrative to the myths of Whiteness" since at least the 1840s—to a generally disinterested white audience.[14] And for all of their increased visibility, critical perspectives on whiteness today find as many opponents as they do supporters and struggle to keep whiteness visible in the long term.

The question of how to make whiteness strange, then, is still not settled. Nor is it universally accepted that it needs to be or self-evident what to do with whiteness made strange. In a satirical 1860 article, social commentator William J. Wilson asked, "What shall we do with the white people?" The question was important then, and with good reason, it still keeps being asked.[15] There are several major lines of thought common among white-racialized people that bear mention here:

- *White nationalists and white supremacists*: While color blindness is currently a widespread ideology, overt interpersonal racism and white supremacy are by no means gone. Racist, neo-Nazi, and other white supremacist ideologies still attract followers, and organization in the name of protecting the "white race" from "white genocide" or to further the cause of white supremacy is still common. In cleaned-up forms, such as under labels like "alt-right," "white nationalist," or "national populism," similar ideas are gaining traction in public discourse around the world, and there is significant overlap between overt and covert forms of prowhite activities.

• *Occasionally race-conscious whites*: This line of thought about the future of whiteness can perhaps best be described as a continuation of color blindness. Representatives don't see whiteness as a problematic identity because they don't associate it with power and privilege but rather see it as one form of identity among many. They may identify as white primarily when they encounter critiques of whiteness or are racialized as white. They sometimes proclaim that "it's OK to be white," and perhaps see themselves as being victims of forms of reverse discrimination when they see affirmative action policies or similar measures toward social justice or the redress of inequalities.

• *Reframing advocates*: Others allow for the fact that historically and in the present, whiteness has served as a source of oppression, but hold out hope that it can be redeemed or rehabilitated, or at the very least, that there are aspects of whiteness that can serve positive or constructive purposes. Whiteness here isn't an identity among others. Instead, the argument is that it might one day be. Philosopher Linda Alcoff, for example, argues in her 2015 assessment *The Future of Whiteness* "against the idea that white identity cannot adapt in positive ways to a loss of centrality. It is not at all clear that, without white supremacy, there can be no whiteness."[16] And scholar Veronica T. Watson argues that taking the lessons of the literature of "white estrangement" to heart could "remind Whiteness of choices it *could* make to redeem its past, correct its present, and create a more just future."[17]

• *Whiteness "abolitionists"*: This end of the spectrum includes those who, like education professor Alice McIntyre, would contend that "there *is no positive in whiteness*."[18] The journal *Race Traitor* (1993–2005)—with the tagline "Treason to whiteness is loyalty to humanity," and coedited by academic affairs officer John Garvey and historian Noel Ignatiev—took a clear stance in its first editorial: "The key to solving the social problems of our age is to abolish the white race. Until that task is accomplished, there can be no universal reform, and even partial reform will prove elusive."[19] And starting from Baldwin's observations in "On Being 'White' . . . and Other Lies" (1984), David Roediger tells readers of his *Towards the Abolition of Whiteness* (1994) that "it is not merely that whiteness is oppressive and false; it is that whiteness is *nothing but* oppressive and false."[20]

To "abolitionists," then, whiteness cannot be redeemed, and only when it has withered away can its wrongs and harms be truly faced. Because of its historical foundation in colonialism, imperialism, genocide, and racism, writes Mark LeVine, "one would have better luck taking wetness away from water . . . than to rip the racism out of whiteness."[21]

These categories are ideal types and amalgams, and the perspectives they represent all have their critics, but they show that there is no commonly shared answer to Wilson's question. What will happen to whiteness is still uncertain.[22]

But for advocates of making whiteness strange, whether to transform or abolish it, another burning question remains. Dyer wrote that "there is no more powerful position than that of being 'just' human," a privilege afforded to white people, who are less often raced. The point of seeing "white" people as raced is "to dislodge them/us from the position of power, with all the inequities, oppression, privileges and sufferings in its train, dislodging them/us by undercutting the authority with which they/we act in and on the world."[23] What is at stake, then, when we speak of whiteness rather than about "dominant groups," "hegemonies," or "racialization" processes—all of which are important conceptual tools in their own right—is that it allows us to speak frankly and with specificity about something that gains some of its power from being unnamed: if the dominant group is named in the same way as dominated groups, if hegemonies are labeled by the interests they turn into common sense, if the racializer is also racialized, then we can better engage in critical, antiracist work in academia and beyond.

In response to the ascendance of color blindness, it has become more common to see calls for "race consciousness," which in Michael Omi and Howard Winant's definition "involves *noticing* the social fact of race, the presence of racial identity/difference, racial inequality, and racial hierarchy."[24] This is not a call to reify or biologize race but instead to take it seriously in a radically pragmatic way as a shifting complex of social practices, structures, representations, and self-representations. And it means to acknowledge that although socially constructed, race has real and unequal consequences. Talking about whiteness is crucial in our day and age; time and time again we are reminded of this necessity. If we don't, we'll have much harder time seeing the ways white supremacy works to dominate and oppress, and a far much harder time challenging it.

Whiteness is, has been, and can be many different things. It's been a bribe and bludgeon, a lie and promise. One thing that it is not, though, is neutral. Whether we think of it as a possession or privilege, whiteness is manufactured in the ways described in these pages and many besides. If the racial formation theory at the heart of this book carries any explanatory power, however, something important remains to be said. Scholarship alone cannot undo whiteness. Neither can teaching. You cannot educate away a structure. This is not to say that scholarship, education, knowledge production, or consciousness-raising aren't important. Yet they're a means to an end. "We must develop an epistemology of racial emancipation as the necessary corrective to the racial grammar that fosters and reflects the 'moral economy of whiteness,'" writes Eduardo Bonilla-Silva, then immediately adds, "But please know that epistemology and counter-ideological struggles alone have not liberated anyone in history!"[25] The goal must be to change politics, not attitudes; structures, not individuals. It's not easy, and white people don't need to invent the struggle or seek to lead it. *Nor should we try to*. People racialized as Other to whiteness understand the effects and consequences of whiteness better than we ever can. But we can't stand by on the sidelines anymore either.

Activism and organization might also not be enough in the end, but they carry a far greater potential than teaching and learning alone. Nobody can do everything, but everyone can do something. "Just as there are millions of us fighting," write editor Akiba Solomon and journalist Kenrya Rankin about Black US American resistance and subversion of white supremacy, "there are millions

You cannot educate away a structure. . . . The goal must be to change politics, not attitudes; structures, not individuals.

of ways to land blows."[26] If this book has made whiteness strange to you, keep talking about it with those around you to whom it remains "natural." If this book has made whiteness strange to you, keep thinking about it and seek out ways to help dismantle white supremacy. If this book has made whiteness strange to you, strive never to forget that nothing about whiteness is neutral. And find the best way for you to land blows.

ACKNOWLEDGMENTS

I want to thank the three anonymous reviewers who read this manuscript; I can't put into words how grateful I am for their close, careful, and critical readings! Thanks to the many colleagues, students, and friends who have talked and thought about whiteness with me over the past decade. There's too many of you to name but if this description fits you, know that I appreciate you more than words can say. Sean Guynes co-laid the foundations for and co-created the structure of *Whiteness*. The book wouldn't exist without him, but all its errors are mine. Jonas Otterbeck first introduced me to critical whiteness studies, and for that I am eternally grateful. Matthew Teutsch was a constant conversation partner throughout the writing process, read parts of the text, and offered helpful suggestions. Andie Alexander was asked to put together the book's index at the eleventh hour, and did so with a keen eye and an artist's hand. If it weren't for the incredible work, support, help, and understanding offered by the MIT Press's Matthew Browne and Deborah M. Cantor-Adams, I'm not sure this book would have ever been completed. And Jordan—I owe you *everything!*

GLOSSARY

Hegemony
The relatively dominant position of a group or idea over others, often supported by norms and other social, cultural, ideological, economic, or political factors. Hegemonic ideas tend to become framed as "common sense," which makes it harder for other ideas to be disseminated, but hegemonies are never unchallenged or universally accepted.

Racial formation
A sociohistorical process in which racial classifications and identities are created, lived out, transformed, and destroyed via social, economic, and political forces.

Racialization
The process of ascribing racial meaning onto groups or individuals.

Racism
Popularly understood as averse personal opinions or bias about people of color, but more commonly conceptualized in scholarship and activism as a racial power structure that puts one group at a particular advantage while disadvantaging other groups.

Western
A geopolitical designation that usually encompasses North America and Europe. Rather than being purely geographic, the term also carries assumptions about culture and society that exclude Indigenous peoples in the Americas, Australia, and northern Europe, for example. The term often implies whiteness or is used as a near synonym.

White fragility
An intense reaction to being racialized as white, frequently characterized by defensiveness, evasions, or recriminations that cut short discussions about race, and thus serve to maintain white supremacy.

White genocide
A conspiracy theory that centers on the claim that the future of white people is being threatened by "deliberate design." Sometimes also called the Great Replacement.

White guilt
Typically refers to a sense of guilt felt by or attributed to white people over the historical crimes committed by and privileges extended to white people over and against people of color.

White privilege
The accrued historical benefits afforded to white and white-passing people in racist and white supremacist societies on the basis of whiteness.

White rage
The effort to curtail the ambitions, demands, and advances of people of color in white supremacist societies through legislation, policy, and other repressive means.

White supremacy
A multifaceted term that can refer to the ideology or belief that white people are inherently superior, a social or political system of white domination, or a sociopolitical paradigm that promotes and upholds white supremacist ideals, beliefs, and politics.

Whiteness
A racial formation that functions as system of social control.

NOTES

Chapter 1

1. I use "US American" when referring to something pertaining to the United States rather than the more common "American." The latter normalizes the imperialist notion that the United States is *the* "America" instead of one part of the Americas. The usage also owes to Toni Morrison's observation that "American means white." Toni Morrison, *Playing in the Dark: Whiteness and the Literary Imagination* (New York: Vintage Books, 1993), 47.

2. International opposition to apartheid was mobilized since at least 1960, following the Sharpeville Massacre in March of that year where white police fired into a crowd and killed or injured hundreds of Black South Africans. See Elizabeth M. Williams, *The Politics of Race in Britain and South Africa: Black British Solidarity and the Anti-Apartheid Struggle* (London: I. B. Tauris, 2015) for examples of how white British resistance to apartheid didn't always translate to opposition to racism in the UK.

3. The "think they are white" phrasing comes from James Baldwin, "On Being 'White' . . . and Other Lies" (1984), in *The Cross of Redemption: Uncollected Writings*, ed. Randall Kenan (New York: Pantheon Books, 2010), 137.

4. Cf. Steve Garner, *Whiteness: An Introduction* (London: Routledge, 2007), 11.

5. John Jennings, foreword to Frederick Luis Aldama, *Latinx Superheroes in Mainstream Comics* (Tucson: University of Arizona Press, 2017), xi.

6. Reni Eddo-Lodge, *Why I'm No Longer Talking to White People about Race* (London: Bloomsbury Publishing, 2018), xvii.

7. Eduardo Bonilla-Silva, *Racism without Racists: Color-blind Racism and the Persistence of Racial Inequality in America*, 4th ed. (Lanham, MD: Rowman and Littlefield, 2014), 151.

8. Bonilla-Silva, *Racism without Racists*, 171.

9. Nathan Glazer and Daniel P. Moynihan, *Beyond the Melting Pot: The Negroes, Puerto Ricans, Jews, Italians, and Irish of New York City* (Cambridge, MA: MIT Press, 1970), 23.

10. Tressie McMillan Cottom, *Thick: And Other Essays* (New York: New Press, 2019), 112.

Chapter 2

1. Michael Omi and Howard Winant, *Racial Formation in the United States*, 3rd ed. (New York: Routledge, 2015), 109.

2. Theodore Allen, *The Invention of the White Race, Volume I: Racial Oppression and Social Control*, 2nd ed. (London: Verso, 2012), 22.

3. Omi and Winant, *Racial Formation*, 124, 125 (emphasis in original).

4. Cf. Peter Wikström and Tobias Hübinette, "Equality Data as Immoral Race Politics: A Case Study of Liberal, Colour-Blind, and Antiracialist Opposition to Equality Data in Sweden," *British Journal of Social Psychology* (2021): 1154–1176. Discussing resistance in Sweden to collecting equality data, the authors argue that owing in part to "hegemonic Swedish colour-blind antiracialism, there is no officially or publicly acceptable language for talking about race in Swedish" (1158).

5. Omi and Winant, *Racial Formation*, 109.

6. Omi and Winant, *Racial Formation*, 128 (emphasis in original).

7. Richard Dyer, *The Matter of Images: Essays on Representation*, 2nd ed. (London: Routledge, 2002), 51.

8. Achille Mbembe, *Critique of Black Reason*, trans. Laurent Dubois (Durham, NC: Duke University Press, 2017), 43.

9. Cf. Sven Lindqvist, *The Dead Do Not Die: "Exterminate All the Brutes" and Terra Nullius*, trans. Joan Tate and Sarah Death (New York: Free Press, 2014), 107–108.

10. George M. Fredrickson, *Racism: A Short History* (Princeton, NJ: Princeton University Press, 2002), 40–41.

11. In Genesis 9:20–29, it is Ham's son Shem who is cursed, but the curse was generally named after the father.

12. On the complicated history of the curse of Ham and its uses, see David M. Goldenberg, *Black and Slave: The Origins and History of the Curse of Ham* (Berlin: Walter de Gruyter, 2017).

13. Elin Lena Labba, *Herrarna satte oss hit: om tvångsförflyttningarna i Sverige* (Stockholm: Nordstedts, 2020).

14. Omi and Winant, *Racial Formation*, 112–115.

15. Cf. Nell Irvin Painter, *The History of White People* (New York: W. W. Norton, 2011), chap. 3; Allen, *Invention of the White Race, Volume I*.

16. This shift and its prehistory are chronicled in detail in Theodore Allen, *The Invention of the White Race, Volume II: The Origin of Racial Oppression in Anglo-America*, 2nd ed. (London: Verso, 2012).

17. Allen, *Invention of the White Race, Volume I*, 184.

18. Painter, *History of White People*, 107.

19. Allen, *Invention of the White Race, Volume II*, 33.

20. Painter, *History of White People*, 79.

21. Fredrickson, *Racism*, 100–101.

22. Fredrickson, *Racism*, 2.

23. Cf. Edward Telles and René Flores, "Not Just Color: Whiteness, Nation, and Status in Latin America," *Hispanic American Historical Review* 93, no. 3 (2013): 411–449.

24. Allen, *Invention of the White Race, Volume I*, back cover.

25. See, for example, Sven Lindqvist's *Terra Nullius*, reprinted in Lindqvist, *Dead Do Not Die*, 187–382.

26. Michelle Alexander, *The New Jim Crow: Mass Incarceration in the Age of Colorblindness* (New York: New Press, 2011); Matthew Frye Jacobson, *Roots Too: White Ethnic Revival in Post–Civil Rights America* (Cambridge, MA: Harvard University Press, 2008).

27. Cf. Gabriel Kuhn, *Liberating Sápmi: Indigenous Resistance in Europe's Far North* (Oakland, CA: PM Press, 2019); Labba, *Herrarna satte oss hit*.

28. Catrin Lundström and Tobias Hübinette, *Vit melankoli: En analys av en nation i kris* (Göteborg, Sweden: Makadam förlag, 2020), 58–59.

29. Veronica T. Watson, *The Souls of White Folk: African American Writers Theorize Whiteness* (Jackson: University Press of Mississippi, 2013), 4–5.

30. Cf. Jennifer M. Schmidt and Mary West, "Whiteness Studies in South African Literature: A Bibliography," *English in Africa* 37, no. 1 (2010): 103–114.

31. Cf. Tobias Hübinette, *Att skriva om svenskheten: Studier i de svenska rasrelationerna speglade genom den icke-vita svenska litteraturen* (Malmö, Sweden: Arx förlag, 2019).

Chapter 3

1. Peggy McIntosh, "White Privilege and Male Privilege: A Personal Account of Coming to See Correspondences through Women's Studies" (Wellesley, MA: Wellesley College, Center for Research on Women, 1988), 2.

2. Paul Lappalainen, "Det blågula glashuset—strukturell diskriminering i Sverige" (Stockholm: Statens offentliga utredningar, 2005), 448 (my translation).

3. Ibram X. Kendi, *How to Be an Antiracist* (London: Bodley Head, 2020), 21–22.

4. Nada Hassanein, "Native Americans Die Younger, CDC Study Shows. They Say It's Proof of 'Ongoing Systemic Harm,'" *USA Today*, November 23, 2021, https://eu.usatoday.com/story/news/health/2021/11/23/native-americans-life -expectancy-cdc/6360395001.

5. Australian Institute of Health and Welfare, "Indigenous Life Expectancy and Deaths," in *Australia's Health 2020*, July 23, 2020, https://www.aihw.gov .au/reports/australias-health/indigenous-life-expectancy-and-deaths.

6. On the Islam-centeredness of the "radicalization" framework, see Arun Kundnani, "Radicalisation: The Journey of a Concept," *Race and Class* 54, no. 2 (October 2012): 3–25. On the imbrication of race in the "terrorist" label, see Atiya Husain, "Deracialization, Dissent, and Terrorism in the FBI's Most Wanted Program," *Sociology of Race and Ethnicity* 7, no. 2 (2021): 208–225.

7. Steve Garner, *Whiteness: An Introduction* (London: Routledge, 2007), 17.

8. Charles W. Mills, *The Racial Contract* (Ithaca, NY: Cornell University Press, 1997), 11.

9. McIntosh, "White Privilege and Male Privilege," 3.

10. Cf. Erin Cooley, Jazmin Brown-Iannuzzi, and D'Jonita Cottrell, "Liberals Perceive More Racism Than Conservatives When Police Shoot Black Men—but, Reading about White Privilege Increases Perceived Racism, and Shifts Attributions of Guilt, Regardless of Political Ideology," *Journal of Experimental Social Psychology* 85 (November 2019): 1–9.

11. Fredrik deBoer, "Admitting That White Privilege Helps You Is Really Just Congratulating Yourself," *Washington Post*, January 28, 2016, https://www.washingtonpost.com/posteverything/wp/2016/01/28/when-white-people-admit-white-privilege-theyre-really-just-congratulating-themselves.

12. James Baldwin, "The White Man's Guilt," in *Collected Essays* (New York: Library of America, 1998), 722.

13. Patrick R. Grzanka, Keri A. Frantell, and Ruth E. Fassinger, "The White Racial Affect Scale (WRAS): A Measure of White Guilt, Shame, and Negation," *Counseling Psychologist* 48, no. 1 (January 2020): 47–77.

14. Kyle Smith, "The White-Guilt Cult: A Look at Woke Religiosity," *New Republic*, June 18, 2020, https://www.nationalreview.com/magazine/2020/07/06/the-white-guilt-cult/#slide-1.

15. John Battersby, "Admitting White Guilt," *World Today*, June 1997, 24.

16. Shelby Steele, "White Guilt," *American Scholar* 59, no. 4 (1990): 501.

17. Audre Lorde, *The Master's Tools Will Never Dismantle the Master's House* (Milton Keynes, UK: Penguin Books, 2017), 31.

18. Battersby, "Admitting White Guilt," 23, 25.

19. Clint van der Walt, Vijé Franchi, and Garth Stevens, "The South African Truth and Reconciliation Commission: 'Race,' Historical Compromise and Transitional Democracy," *International Journal of Intercultural Relations* 27, no. 2 (March 2003): 251–267.

20. Antony Sguazzin, "South Africa Wealth Gap Unchanged Since Apartheid, Says World Inequality Lab," *TIME*, August 5, 2021, https://time.com/6087699/south-africa-wealth-gap-unchanged-since-apartheid.

21. Lorde, *Master's Tools*, 30.

22. Robin J. DiAngelo, *White Fragility: Why It's So Hard for White People to Talk about Racism* (Boston: Beacon Press, 2018), 2.

23. DiAngelo, *White Fragility*, 143–144.

24. David Roediger, "On the Defensive: Navigating White Advantage and White Fragility," *Los Angeles Review of Books*, September 6, 2018, https://lareviewofbooks.org/article/on-the-defensive-navigating-white-advantage-and-white-fragility.

25. Austin Channing Brown, *I'm Still Here: Black Dignity in a World Made for Whiteness* (New York: Convergent Books, 2018), 89.

26. DiAngelo, *White Fragility*, 144.

27. J. C. Pan, "Why Diversity Training Isn't Enough," *New Republic*, January 7, 2020, https://newrepublic.com/article/156032/diversity-training-isnt-enough-pamela-newkirk-robin-diangelo-books-reviews.

28. Jonathan Capehart, "From 'White Fragility' to 'White Rage': The Broken Promise of America," *Washington Post*, June 18, 2020, https://www.washingtonpost.com/opinions/2020/06/18/white-fragility-white-rage-broken-promise-america.

29. The term had been used before, such as in Martin Durham's 2007 *White Rage: The Extreme Right and American Politics*, but then in a very different context.

30. Carol Anderson, *White Rage: The Unspoken Truth of Our Racial Divide* (New York: Bloomsbury, 2017), 2.

31. Tobias Hübinette, "De icke-vita väljarna avgjorde det amerikanska presidentvalet och kan också komma att avgöra 2022 års svenska riksdagsval," *Tobias Hübinette*, November 14, 2020, https://tobiashubinette.wordpress.com/2020/11/14/de-icke-vita-valjarna-avgjorde-det-amerikanska-presidentvalet-och-kan-ocksa-komma-att-avgora-2022-ars-svenska-riksdagsval.

32. George M. Fredrickson, *Racism: A Short History* (Princeton, NJ: Princeton University Press, 2002), 75.

33. Quoted in Katherine Botterill and Kathy Burrell, "(In)visibility, Privilege and the Performance of Whiteness in Brexit Britain: Polish Migrants in Britain's Shifting Migration Regime," *Environment and Planning C: Politics and Space* 37, no. 1 (February 2019): 27.

34. Zygmunt Bauman, *Strangers at Our Door* (Cambridge, UK: Polity, 2016), 12–16.

35. Bauman, *Strangers at Our Door*, 14.

36. Tressie McMillan Cottom, *Thick: And Other Essays* (New York: New Press, 2019), 117.

37. David Lane, "White Genocide Manifesto," davidlane1488.com, n.d. https://web.archive.org/web/20191001213058/https://www.davidlane1488.com/whitegenocide.html.

38. Quoted in Jacob Davey and Julia Ebner, "'The Great Replacement': The Violent Consequences of Mainstreamed Extremism" (London: Institute for Strategic Dialogue, 2019), 16.

39. Nell Irvin Painter, *The History of White People* (New York: W. W. Norton, 2011), 250–251.

40. Painter, *History of White People*, 306–307.

41. Douglas Murray, *The Strange Death of Europe: Immigration, Identity, Islam* (London: Bloomsbury Continuum, 2017), 1.

42. Bridge Initiative Team, "Factsheet: White Genocide Conspiracy Theory," Bridge, February 3, 2020, https://bridge.georgetown.edu/research/factsheet-white-genocide-conspiracy-theory.

43. Robert A. Pape and Chicago Project on Security and Threats, "Understanding American Domestic Terrorism: Mobilization Potential and Risk Factors of a New Threat Trajectory," Division of Social Sciences, University of Chicago, April 6, 2021, https://d3qi0qp55mx5f5.cloudfront.net/cpost/i/docs/americas_insurrectionists_online_2021_04_06.pdf?mtime=1617807009.

44. George M. Fredrickson, *White Supremacy: A Comparative Study in American and South African History* (New York: Oxford University Press, 1981), xi.

45. Mills, *Racial Contract*, 1, 12, 11.

46. Mills, *Racial Contract*, 17–18.

Chapter 4

1. Kimberlé W. Crenshaw, "Demarginalizing the Intersection of Race and Sex: A Black Feminist Critique of Antidiscrimination Doctrine, Feminist Theory, and Antiracist Politics," *University of Chicago Legal Forum* 1989, no. 1 (1989): 139–167.

2. Michel Foucault, *The History of Sexuality—Volume 1: An Introduction* (New York: Pantheon Books, 1978), 139.

3. Stefan Kühl, *For the Betterment of the Race: The Rise and Fall of the International Movement for Eugenics and Racial Hygiene*, trans. Lawrence Schofer (New York: Palgrave Macmillan, 2013), 2.

4. Dorothy Roberts, "White Privilege and the Biopolitics of Race," *Understanding and Dismantling Privilege* 1, no. 1 (2010): 3.

5. For a primer, see Ayah Nuriddin, Graham Mooney, and Alexandre I. R. White, "Reckoning with Histories of Medical Racism and Violence in the USA," *Lancet* 396, no. 10256 (October 3, 2020): 949–951.

6. For a thorough account of the ongoing history and salience of "race science," see Angela Saini, *Superior: The Return of Race Science* (London: 4th Estate, 2020).

7. Torbjörn Tännsjö, "Det är inte fel att vilja ha perfekta människor," *Aftonbladet*, October 23, 2009, https://www.aftonbladet.se/a/4dEwLG.

8. Richard Dawkins, Twitter post, February 16, 2020, 8:26 a.m., https://twitter.com/RichardDawkins/status/1228943686953664512.

9. Chanda Prescod-Weinstein, "Stop Equating 'Science' with Truth," *Slate*, August 9, 2017, https://slate.com/technology/2017/08/evolutionary-psychology-is-the-most-obvious-example-of-how-science-is-flawed.html.

10. Nancy Isenberg, *White Trash: The 400-Year Untold History of Class in America* (New York: Viking, 2016), 247ff., 12.

11. Quoted in Ronald T. Takaki, *A Different Mirror: A History of Multicultural America* (New York: Little, Brown and Company, 2008), 58.

12. Michelle Alexander, *The New Jim Crow: Mass Incarceration in the Age of Colorblindness* (New York: New Press, 2011), 25.

13. Cheryl L. Harris, "Whiteness as Property," *Harvard Law Review* 106, no. 9 (1993): 1707–1791.

14. Quoted in Harris, "Whiteness as Property," 1742.

15. George Lipsitz, *The Possessive Investment in Whiteness: How White People Profit from Identity Politics*, 20th anniversary ed. (Philadelphia: Temple University Press, 2018), vii.

16. Håkan Blomqvist, *Nation, ras och civilisation i svensk arbetarrörelse före nazismen* (Stockholm: Carlsson, 2006), 377 (my translation).

17. Catrin Lundström and Tobias Hübinette, *Vit melankoli: En analys av en nation i kris* (Göteborg, Sweden: Makadam förlag, 2020), 25–36.

18. Lipsitz, *Possessive Investment*, xxvii.

19. Niklas Orrenius and Barzan Dello, "Protestupprop mot rasism på Sveriges Radio i BLM-rörelsens spår," *Dagens Nyheter*, September 25, 2020, https://www.dn.se/kultur/protestupprop-mot-rasism-pa-sveriges-radio-i-blm-rorelsens-spar.

20. Kristin McMillen and Anna-Maria Carnhede, "SR tystar medarbetare som skrev under upprop mot rasism," *ETC*, February 2, 2021, https://www.etc.se/kultur-noje/sr-tystar-medarbetare-som-skrev-under-upprop-mot-rasism.

21. Daniel Suhonen, Göran Therborn, and Jesper Weithz, eds., *Klass i Sverige: Ojämlikheten, makten och politiken i det 21:a århundradet* (Lund, Sweden: Arkiv Förlag/Katalys, 2021).

22. David Roediger, *The Sinking Middle Class: A Political History* (New York: O/R Books, 2020), 8.

23. Tressie McMillan Cottom, *Thick: And Other Essays* (New York: New Press, 2019), 124.

24. Roediger, *Sinking Middle Class*, 251–252.

25. Reni Eddo-Lodge, *Why I'm No Longer Talking to White People about Race* (London: Bloomsbury Publishing, 2018), 202.

26. Andrew McCormick, "Madness on Capitol Hill," *Nation*, January 7, 2021, https://www.thenation.com/article/politics/capitol-trump-insurrection-explosions.

27. George M. Fredrickson, *Racism: A Short History* (Princeton, NJ: Princeton University Press, 2002), 61.

28. World Health Organization, "Mercury in Skin Lightening Products" (Geneva: World Health Organization, 2019), 1.

29. David R. Roediger, *Working toward Whiteness: How America's Immigrants Became White. The Strange Journey from Ellis Island to the Suburbs* (New York: Basic Books, 2005), 184–191.

30. Riv-Ellen Prell, *Fighting to Become Americans: Jews, Gender, and the Anxiety of Assimilation* (Boston: Beacon Press, 1999).

31. Mikki Kendall, foreword to Vron Ware, *Beyond the Pale: White Women, Racism, and History*, new ed. (London: Verso, 2015), xii.

32. Charles M. Blow, "How White Women Use Themselves as Instruments of Terror," *New York Times*, May 28, 2020, https://www.nytimes.com/2020/05/27/opinion/racism-white-women.html.

33. Cf. Susan Faludi, *The Terror Dream: Fear and Fantasy in Post-9/11 America* (New York: Metropolitan Books, 2007).

34. See, for example, Shabana Mir, "How Not to Rescue Muslim Women," *Religion Dispatches*, April 16, 2009, https://religiondispatches.org/how-not-to-rescue-muslim-women; Shelina Kassam, "Feminists as 'Saviors' of Muslim Women: The Tension between Gender Equality and Religious Rights," *Bloomsbury Religion in North America* (2021); Shahed Eazydi and Hayfaa Chalabi, "Why Is White Feminism Propping up Hijab Bans in Europe?," *Shado Magazine*, August 22, 2021, https://shado-mag.com/all/why-is-white-feminism-propping-up-hijab-bans-in-europe.

35. Lisa Röstlund and Erik Wikman, "Chatten avslöjar: Rasism, sexism—och krossade hjärtan," *Soldiers of Odin inifrån*, https://soldiersofodin.story.aftonbladet.se/chapter/rasism-och-sexism.

36. Ware, *Beyond the Pale*, xx.

37. Koa Beck, *White Feminism* (New York: Simon and Schuster), 2021), xvii–xviii.

38. Lundström and Hübinette, *Vit melankoli*, 47, 64–65.

39. See, for example, R. W. Connell, *Masculinities*. (Cambridge, UK: Polity, 2005).

40. Michael S. Kimmel, *Angry White Men: American Masculinity at the End of an Era* (New York: Nation Books, 2013), 32, 21–27, 15.

41. Cf. Lundström and Hübinette, *Vit melankoli*, 66–68.

42. Lundström and Hübinette, *Vit melankoli*, 70–74.

43. Richard Dyer, *White* (New York: Routledge, 1997), 30.

Chapter 5

1. Eduardo Bonilla-Silva, "The Invisible Weight of Whiteness: The Racial Grammar of Everyday Life in Contemporary America," *Ethnic and Racial Studies* 35, no. 2 (2012): 174.

2. Michael Omi and Howard Winant, *Racial Formation in the United States*, 3rd ed. (New York: Routledge, 2015), 263.

3. Ebony Elizabeth Thomas, *The Dark Fantastic: Race and the Imagination from Harry Potter to the Hunger Games* (New York: NYU Press, 2019), 5.

4. Debbie Reese, "An Indigenous Critique of Whiteness in Children's Literature," *Children and Libraries* 17, no. 3 (August 30, 2019): 6.

5. Centre for Literacy in Primary Education, "Reflecting Realities: Survey of Ethnic Representation within UK Children's Literature 2018" (London: Centre for Literacy in Primary Education, 2019).

6. Svenska barnboksinstitutet, "Bokprovning på Svenska barnboksinstitutet: en dokumentation" (Stockholm: Svenska barnboksinstitutet, 2019), 13–14.

7. Svenska barnboksinstitutet, "Bokprovning," 12 (my translation).

8. Thomas, *Dark Fantastic*, 5–6.

9. Brynn F. Welch, "The Pervasive Whiteness of Children's Literature: Collective Harms and Consumer Obligations," *Social Theory and Practice* 42, no. 2 (2016): 367–388.

10. Centre for Literacy in Primary Education, "Reflecting Realities," 8.

11. Nancy Larrick, "The All-White World of Children's Books," *Saturday Review*, 1965.

12. Charles W. Mills, *The Racial Contract* (Ithaca, NY: Cornell University Press, 1997), 18.

13. Graeme McMillan, "Are American Comics Institutionally Racist?," *Gizmodo*, April 9, 2009, https://gizmodo.com/are-american-comics-institutionally-racist-5349421.

14. Cf. Richard Dyer, *White* (New York: Routledge, 1997), 39.

15. For details, see Martin Lund, *Re-Constructing the Man of Steel: Superman 1938–1941, Jewish American History, and the Invention of the Jewish-Comics Connection* (New York: Palgrave Macmillan, 2016).

16. In a similar vein, many female superheroes around this time were saddled with infantilizing names; the *Fantastic Four*'s Susan Storm went by Invisible Girl and the *X-Men*'s Jean Grey went by Marvel Girl. While both presented as younger than Storm and Grey, teenagers Peter Parker and Bobby Drake were called Spider-Man and Ice Man, respectively.

17. Kenneth Ghee, "'Will the "Real" Black Superheroes Please Stand Up?!': A Critical Analysis of the Mythological and Cultural Significance of Black Superheroes," in *Black Comics: Politics of Race and Representation*, ed. Sheena L. Howard and Ronald L. Jackson II (London: Bloomsbury, 2013), 232.

18. Cf. Consuela Francis, "American Truths: Blackness and the American Superhero," in *The Blacker the Ink: Constructions of Black Identity in Comics and Sequential Art*, ed. Frances K. Gateward and John Jennings (New Brunswick, NJ: Rutgers University Press, 2015), 150; Albert S. Fu, "Fear of a Black Spider-Man: Racebending and the Colour-Line in Superhero (Re)Casting," *Journal of Graphic Novels and Comics* 6, no. 3 (July 3, 2015): 269–283.

19. Francis, "American Truths," 140.

20. Jeff Yang, Parry Shen, Keith Chow, and Jerry Ma, eds., *Secret Identities: The Asian American Superhero Anthology* (New York: New Press, 2009).

21. Siri Srinivas, "Super Sikh: A Superhero in a Turban Fighting Injustice and Ignorance," *Guardian*, March 9, 2015, https://www.theguardian.com/books/2015/mar/09/super-sikh-comic-book-superhero.

22. Reprinted in John Ney Rieber, Chuck Austen, John Cassaday, Trevor Hairsine, and Jae Lee, *Captain America: Marvel Knights. Vol. 1* (New York: Marvel, 2016). Captain America can be considered a "walking, talking, (near) indestructible symbol of American courage, strength, and virtue," notes Francis ("American Truths," 139). As such, the character exemplifies other ways that superhero narratives can neutralize critique and rehabilitate whiteness despite opposing racism. For more examples, see Francis, "American Truths"; Osvaldo Oyola, "Marked for Failure: Whiteness, Innocence, and Power in Defining Captain America," in *Unstable Masks: Whiteness and American Superhero Comics*, ed. Sean Guynes and Martin Lund (Columbus: Ohio State University, 2020), 19–37.

23. Marc Singer, "'Black Skins' and White Masks: Comic Books and the Secret of Race," *African American Review* 36, no. 1 (2002): 110.

24. Ruth Frankenberg, *White Women, Race Matters: The Social Construction of Whiteness* (London: Routledge, 1993), 36.

25. Osvaldo Oyola, "'Say It Loud!' Tyroc and the Trajectory of the Black Superhero (Part 1)," *Middle Spaces* (blog), November 3, 2020, https://themiddlespaces.com/2020/11/03/say-it-loud-tyroc-pt1.

26. Reprinted in Aaron McGruder, *A Right to Be Hostile: The Boondocks Treasury* (New York: Three Rivers Press, 2003), 42.

27. Gary R. Edgerton, *The Columbia History of American Television* (New York: Columbia University Press, 2007), 244.

28. Paul Chidester, "May the Circle Stay Unbroken: *Friends*, the Presence of Absence, and the Rhetorical Reinforcement of Whiteness," *Critical Studies in Media Communication* 25, no. 2 (2009): 161.

29. The more recent sitcom titled *The Goldbergs* (2013–) is unrelated to the older series.

30. Amanda Dyanne Lotz, "Segregated Sitcoms: Institutional Causes of Disparity among Black and White Comedy Images and Audiences," in *The Sitcom Reader: America View and Skewed*, ed. Mary M. Dalton and Laura R. Linder (Albany: SUNY Press, 2005), 146.

31. Quoted in Lotz, "Segregated Sitcoms," 140.

32. Michael Real and Lauren Bratslavsky, "*The Cosby Show*: Recoding Ethnicity and Masculinity within the Television Text," in *The Sitcom Reader: America Re-Viewed, Still Skewed*, ed. Mary M. Dalton and Laura R. Linder (Albany: SUNY Press, 2016), 151–152, 160.

33. Lotz, "Segregated Sitcoms," 145.

34. Cf. Naomi R. Rockler, "*Friends*, Judaism, and the Holiday Armadillo: Mapping a Rhetoric of Postidentity Politics," *Communication Theory* 16 (2006): 454.

35. Taylor Nygaard and Jorie Lagerwey, *Horrible White People: Gender, Genre, and Television's Precarious Whiteness* (New York: NYU Press, 2020), 48.

36. Cf. Nygaard and Lagerwey, *Horrible White People*, 44–46, 50–51, 58.

37. Starting out, actress, writer, and producer Issa Rae was told that "if you want this shit to set off to the next level, you got to put a white character in there, then white people will care about it, then NPR is going to write about your shit, and it'll blow up," which first seemed like a self-fulfilling prophecy. Developing *Insecure*, a comedy-drama show she wrote and starred in, she initially followed the same advice but soon began resisting the push to create a "bridge" to white viewers. Having stopped trying to cater to white audiences, she found "realized, 'Oh my gosh, our show is just about Black characters now in the most refreshing way.'" See Jamal Jordan, "Issa Rae and the New Rules of Black TV," *MIC*, June 10, 2021, https://www.mic.com/culture/issa-rae-cover-story-october-2021.

38. Rockler, "*Friends*, Judaism, and the Holiday Armadillo," 158.

39. Darnell Hunt and Ana-Christina Ramón, "Hollywood Diversity Report 2020: A Tale of Two Hollywoods. Part 2: Television" (Los Angeles: UCLA College of Social Sciences, 2020), https://socialsciences.ucla.edu/hollywood

-diversity-report-2020. These aren't sitcoms alone, but related programming to some extent follows the same general trends.

40. Creative Diversity Network, "Race and Ethnic Diversity: A Deep Dive into Diamond Data" (London: Creative Diversity Network, October 2020), https://creativediversitynetwork.com/wp-content/uploads/2020/10/RED-Full -Report-121020.pdf.

41. Bim Adewunmi, "Why Black British Drama Is Going Online, Not on TV," *Guardian*, July 2, 2012, http://www.theguardian.com/world/2012/jul/02 /black-british-tv-drama-online.

42. Lotz, "Segregated Sitcoms," 148.

43. Hunt and Ramón, "Hollywood Diversity Report," 81–82.

44. Bonilla-Silva, "Invisible Weight of Whiteness," 180.

Chapter 6

1. George M. Fredrickson, *Racism: A Short History* (Princeton, NJ: Princeton University Press, 2002), 4.

2. Robin J. DiAngelo, *White Fragility: Why It's So Hard for White People to Talk about Racism* (Boston: Beacon Press, 2018), 72.

3. Paul Lappalainen, "Det blågula glashuset—Strukturell diskriminering i sverige" (Stockholm: Statens offentliga utredningar, 2005), 31.

4. Catrin Lundström and Tobias Hübinette, *Vit melankoli: En analys av en nation i kris* (Göteborg, Sweden: Makadam förlag, 2020), 56.

5. Teun A. van Dijk, *Discourse and Power* (New York: Palgrave Macmillan, 2008), 123–124.

6. Michael Omi and Howard Winant, *Racial Formation in the United States*, 3rd ed. (New York: Routledge, 2015), 2.

7. Lundström and Hübinette, *Vit melankoli*, 40.

8. Some consequences of this were made visible to white Sweden in summer 2021. Among the things discussed was that many children were taken without parental consent and that many adopted Swedes face the exact racism that adoption was supposed to disprove.

9. Charles Gallagher and France Winddance Twine, "From Wave to Tsunami: The Growth of Third Wave Whiteness," *Ethnic and Racial Studies* 40, no. 9 (2017): 1602.

10. Ibram X. Kendi, *How to Be an Antiracist* (London: Bodley Head, 2020), 10.

11. Eduardo Bonilla-Silva, *Racism without Racists: Color-blind Racism and the Persistence of Racial Inequality in America*, 4th ed. (Lanham, MD: Rowman and Littlefield, 2014), 2.

12. Bonilla-Silva, *Racism without Racists*, chap. 3.

13. Omi and Winant, *Racial Formation*, 264.

14. Omi and Winant, *Racial Formation*, 203–204.

15. Cheryl L. Harris, "Whiteness as Property," *Harvard Law Review* 106, no. 9 (1993): 1777.

16. Mattias Karlsson and David Lång, "Intensifierat arbete mot svenskfientlighet," *Riksdagen*, 2013, https://www.riksdagen.se/sv/webb-tv/video/motion/intensifierat-arbete-mot-svenskfientlighet_H102A353; Daniel Vergara, "Nytt SD-initiativ—'Förenar dem med vit makt-miljön,'" Expo.se, November 2, 2020, https://expo.se/2020/11/nytt-sd-initiativ-%E2%80%9Df%C3%B6renar -dem-med-vit-makt-milj%C3%B6n%E2%80%9D.

17. Matthew Frye Jacobson, *Roots Too: White Ethnic Revival in Post–Civil Rights America* (Cambridge, MA: Harvard University Press, 2008), 359.

18. Quoted in Kuba Shand-Baptiste, "Opinion: The Government Is Not Taking Racism Seriously and Uses MPs of Colour to Avoid Criticism," *Independent*, October 22, 2020, https://www.independent.co.uk/voices/critical-race-theory -racism-kemi-badenoch-black-history-month-bame-discrimination-b1227367 .html.

19. "Le manifeste des 100," *Le Monde*, November 1, 2020, https://manifest edes90.wixsite.com/monsite (my translation).

20. Valerie Kyeyune Backström, "Om det är detta som krävs är det orimligt," *Expressen*, October 3, 2020, https://www.expressen.se/kultur/bocker/om-det -ar-detta-som-kravs-ar-det-orimligt.

21. Jan Guillou, "Tydligen är jag som vit en mindre önskvärd läsare," *Expressen*, October 11, 2020, https://www.aftonbladet.se/nyheter/kolumnister/a/0Kn 38A/tydligen-ar-jag-som-vit-en-mindre-onskvard-lasare. Here and in the following direct quotes from Guillou's opinion piece, all translations and emphasis are mine.

22. Toni Morrison, *Playing in the Dark: Whiteness and the Literary Imagination* (New York: Vintage Books, 1993), 12.

23. James Baldwin, "Letter from a Region in My Mind," *New Yorker*, November 9, 1962, https://www.newyorker.com/magazine/1962/11/17/letter-from-a -region-in-my-mind.

24. NOFX, "Don't Call Me White," track 5 on *Punk in Drublic* (Los Angeles: Epitaph Records, 1994).

25. Cf. Frye Jacobson, *Roots Too*, 21–22, 197, 243–244.

26. Cf. Karen Brodkin, *How Jews Became White Folks and What That Says about Race in America* (New Brunswick, NJ: Rutgers University Press, 1998).

27. Vandala, "'I Try to Keep Punk Rock Punk. You're Not Getting a Nice Story out of Me.' The Fat Mike Interview," *Vandala* (blog), January 3, 2017,

https://vandalamagazine.com/2017/01/03/i-try-to-keep-punk-rock-punk-youre
-not-getting-a-nice-story-out-of-me-the-fat-mike-interview.

28. George Lipsitz, *The Possessive Investment in Whiteness: How White People Profit from Identity Politics*, 20th anniversary ed. (Philadelphia: Temple University Press, 2018), 21.

29. Hanif Abdurraqib, "I Wasn't Brought Here, I Was Born: Surviving Punk Rock Long Enough to Find Afropunk," *Pitchfork*, August 10, 2015, https://pitchfork.com/thepitch/862-i-wasnt-brought-here-i-was-born-surviving-punk-rock-long-enough-to-find-afropunk.

30. Omi and Winant, *Racial Formation*, 220.

31. Gallagher and Winddance Twine, "From Wave to Tsunami," 1602.

32. Omi and Winant, *Racial Formation*, 263.

Chapter 7

1. Jeangu Macrooy, "I Know My Own Strength and That's What Will Keep Me Going"—the Netherlands' Jeangu Macrooy Discusses His Personal Connection to 'Birth of a New Age,'" interview by Oliver Adams, April 26, 2021, https://wiwibloggs.com/2021/04/26/interview-netherlands-jeangu-macrooy-birth-of-a-new-age/264480.

2. Gloria Wekker, *White Innocence: Paradoxes of Colonialism and Race* (Durham, NC: Duke University Press, 2016).

3. James Baldwin, "The White Man's Guilt," in *Collected Essays* (New York: Library of America, 1998), 723.

4. Sven Lindqvist, *The Dead Do Not Die: "Exterminate All the Brutes" and Terra Nullius*, trans. Joan Tate and Sarah Death (New York: Free Press, 2014), 352.

5. Lindqvist, *Dead Do Not Die*, 177–178.

6. Julian Chambliss, "Don't Call Them Memorials," *Frieze*, August 23, 2017, https://www.frieze.com/article/dont-call-them-memorials.

7. Trump White House, "1776 Commission Takes Historic and Scholarly Step to Restore Understanding of the Greatness of the American Founding," January 18, 2021. https://trumpwhitehouse.archives.gov/briefings-statements/1776-commission-takes-historic-scholarly-step-restore-understanding-great
ness-american-founding.

8. Quoted in Lindqvist, *Dead Do Not Die*, 352.

9. Lindqvist, *Dead Do Not Die*, 353.

10. Richard Dyer, *The Matter of Images: Essays on Representation*, 2nd ed. (London: Routledge, 2002), xiv.

11. Peggy McIntosh, "White Privilege and Male Privilege: A Personal Account of Coming to See Correspondences through Women's Studies" (Wellesley, MA: Wellesley College, Center for Research on Women, 1988), 13.

12. Steve Garner, *Whiteness: An Introduction* (London: Routledge, 2007), 24.

13. Charles Gallagher and France Winddance Twine, "From Wave to Tsunami: The Growth of Third Wave Whiteness," *Ethnic and Racial Studies* 40, no. 9 (2017): 1599.

14. Veronica T. Watson, *The Souls of White Folk: African American Writers Theorize Whiteness* (Jackson: University Press of Mississippi, 2013), 6, 38.

15. See Watson, *Souls of White Folk*, 3.

16. Linda Alcoff, *The Future of Whiteness* (Cambridge, UK: Polity, 2015), 19.

17. Watson, *Souls of White Folk*, 141.

18. Alice McIntyre, "Exploring Whiteness and Multicultural Education with Prospective Teachers," *Curriculum Inquiry* 32, no. 1 (2002): 39.

19. John Garvey and Noel Ignatiev, "Abolish the White Race—by Any Means Necessary," *Race Traitor* 1, no. 1 (1993): 1.

20. David R. Roediger, *Towards the Abolition of Whiteness: Essays on Race, Politics, and Working Class History* (London: Verso, 1994), 13.

21. Mark LeVine, "Abolishing Whiteness Has Never Been More Urgent," *Al Jazeera*, November 17, 2019. https://www.aljazeera.com/opinions/2019/11/17/abolishing-whiteness-has-never-been-more-urgent.

22. For a good overview of several such critiques and additional examples of the above positions, see Peter Kolchin, "Whiteness Studies: The New History of Race in America," *Journal of American History* 89, no. 1 (June 2002): 168–170.

23. Richard Dyer, *White* (New York: Routledge, 1997), 2.

24. Michael Omi and Howard Winant, *Racial Formation in the United States*, 3rd ed. (New York: Routledge, 2015), 260.

25. Eduardo Bonilla-Silva, "The Invisible Weight," of Whiteness: The Racial Grammar of Everyday Life in Contemporary America," *Ethnic and Racial Studies* 35, no. 2 (2012): 187.

26. Akiba Solomon and Kenrya Rankin, eds., *How We Fight White Supremacy: A Field Guide to Black Resistance* (New York: Nation Books, 2019), vii.

BIBLIOGRAPHY

Abdurraqib, Hanif. "I Wasn't Brought Here, I Was Born: Surviving Punk Rock Long Enough to Find Afropunk." *Pitchfork*, August 10, 2015. https://pitchfork .com/thepitch/862-i-wasnt-brought-here-i-was-born-surviving-punk-rock -long-enough-to-find-afropunk.

Adewunmi, Bim. "Why Black British Drama Is Going Online, Not on TV." *Guardian*, July 2, 2012. http://www.theguardian.com/world/2012/jul/02/black -british-tv-drama-online.

Alcoff, Linda. *The Future of Whiteness*. Cambridge, UK: Polity, 2015.

Aldama, Frederick Luis. *Latinx Superheroes in Mainstream Comics*. Tucson: University of Arizona Press, 2017.

Alexander, Michelle. *The New Jim Crow: Mass Incarceration in the Age of Colorblindness*. New York: New Press, 2011.

Allen, Theodore. *The Invention of the White Race, Volume I: Racial Oppression and Social Control*. 2nd ed. London: Verso, 2012.

Allen, Theodore. *The Invention of the White Race, Volume II: The Origin of Racial Oppression in Anglo-America*. 2nd ed. London: Verso, 2012.

Anderson, Carol. *White Rage: The Unspoken Truth of Our Racial Divide*. New York: Bloomsbury, 2017.

Australian Institute of Health and Welfare. "Indigenous Life Expectancy and Deaths." In *Australia's Health 2020*, July 23, 2020. https://www.aihw.gov.au /reports/australias-health/indigenous-life-expectancy-and-deaths.

Baldwin, James. "Letter from a Region in My Mind." *New Yorker*, November 9, 1962. https://www.newyorker.com/magazine/1962/11/17/letter-from-a -region-in-my-mind.

Baldwin, James. "On Being 'White' . . . and Other Lies." In *The Cross of Redemption: Uncollected Writings*, edited by Randall Kenan, 135–138. New York: Pantheon Books, 2010.

Baldwin, James. "The White Man's Guilt." In *Collected Essays*, 722–727. New York: Library of America, 1998.

Battersby, John. "Admitting White Guilt." *World Today*, June 1997.

Bauman, Zygmunt. *Strangers at Our Door*. Cambridge, UK: Polity, 2016.

Beck, Koa. *White Feminism*. New York: Simon and Schuster, 2021.

Blomqvist, Håkan. *Nation, ras och civilisation i svensk arbetarrörelse före nazismen*. Stockholm: Carlsson, 2006.

Blow, Charles M. "How White Women Use Themselves as Instruments of Terror." *New York Times*, May 28, 2020. https://www.nytimes.com/2020/05/27/opinion/racism-white-women.html.

Bonilla-Silva, Eduardo. "The Invisible Weight of Whiteness: The Racial Grammar of Everyday Life in Contemporary America." *Ethnic and Racial Studies* 35, no. 2 (2012): 173–194.

Bonilla-Silva, Eduardo. *Racism without Racists: Color-blind Racism and the Persistence of Racial Inequality in America*. 4th ed. Lanham, MD: Rowman and Littlefield Publishers, Inc, 2014.

Botterill, Katherine, and Kathy Burrell. "(In)visibility, Privilege and the Performance of Whiteness in Brexit Britain: Polish Migrants in Britain's Shifting Migration Regime." *Environment and Planning C: Politics and Space* 37, no. 1 (February 2019): 23–28.

Bridge Initiative Team. "Factsheet: White Genocide Conspiracy Theory." Bridge, February 3, 2020. https://bridge.georgetown.edu/research/factsheet-white-genocide-conspiracy-theory.

Brodkin, Karen. *How Jews Became White Folks and What That Says about Race in America*. New Brunswick, NJ: Rutgers University Press, 1998.

Brown, Austin Channing. *I'm Still Here: Black Dignity in a World Made for Whiteness*. New York: Convergent Books, 2018.

Capehart, Jonathan. "From 'White Fragility' to 'White Rage': The Broken Promise of America." *Washington Post*, June 18, 2020. https://www.washingtonpost.com/opinions/2020/06/18/white-fragility-white-rage-broken-promise-america.

Centre for Literacy in Primary Education. "Reflecting Realities: Survey of Ethnic Representation within UK Children's Literature 2018." London: Centre for Literacy in Primary Education, 2019.

Chambliss, Julian. "Don't Call Them Memorials." *Frieze*, August 23, 2017. https://www.frieze.com/article/dont-call-them-memorials.

Chidester, Paul. "May the Circle Stay Unbroken: *Friends*, the Presence of Absence, and the Rhetorical Reinforcement of Whiteness." *Critical Studies in Media Communication* 25, no. 2 (2009): 157–174.

Connell, R. W. *Masculinities*. Cambridge, UK: Polity, 2005.

Cooley, Erin, Jazmin Brown-Iannuzzi, and D'Jonita Cottrell. "Liberals Perceive More Racism Than Conservatives When Police Shoot Black Men—but, Reading about White Privilege Increases Perceived Racism, and Shifts Attributions of Guilt, Regardless of Political Ideology." *Journal of Experimental Social Psychology* 85 (November 2019): 1–9. https://doi.org/10.1016/j.jesp.2019.103885.

Cottom, Tressie McMillan. *Thick: And Other Essays*. New York: New Press, 2019.

Creative Diversity Network. "Race and Ethnic Diversity: A Deep Dive into Diamond Data." London: Creative Diversity Network, October 2020. https://creativediversitynetwork.com/wp-content/uploads/2020/10/RED-Full-Report-121020.pdf.

Crenshaw, Kimberlé W. "Demarginalizing the Intersection of Race and Sex: A Black Feminist Critique of Antidiscrimination Doctrine, Feminist Theory, and Antiracist Politics." *University of Chicago Legal Forum* 1989, no. 1 (1989): 139–167.

Davey, Jacob, and Julia Ebner. "'The Great Replacement': The Violent Consequences of Mainstreamed Extremism." London: Institute for Strategic Dialogue, 2019.

deBoer, Fredrik. "Admitting That White Privilege Helps You Is Really Just Congratulating Yourself." *Washington Post*, January 28, 2016. https://www.washingtonpost.com/posteverything/wp/2016/01/28/when-white-people-admit-white-privilege-theyre-really-just-congratulating-themselves.

DiAngelo, Robin J. *White Fragility: Why It's So Hard for White People to Talk about Racism*. Boston: Beacon Press, 2018.

Dijk, Teun A. van. *Discourse and Power*. New York: Palgrave Macmillan, 2008.

Dyer, Richard. *The Matter of Images: Essays on Representation*. 2nd ed. London: Routledge, 2002.

Dyer, Richard. *White*. New York: Routledge, 1997.

Eazydi, Shahed, and Hayfaa Chalabi. "Why Is White Feminism Propping up Hijab Bans in Europe?" *Shado Magazine*, August 22, 2021. https://shado-mag .com/all/why-is-white-feminism-propping-up-hijab-bans-in-europe/.

Eddo-Lodge, Reni. *Why I'm No Longer Talking to White People about Race*. London: Bloomsbury Publishing, 2018.

Edgerton, Gary R. *The Columbia History of American Television*. New York: Columbia University Press, 2007.

Faludi, Susan. *The Terror Dream: Fear and Fantasy in Post-9 11 America*. New York: Metropolitan Books, 2007.

Foucault, Michel. *The History of Sexuality—Volume 1: An Introduction*. New York: Pantheon Books, 1978.

Francis, Consuela. "American Truths: Blackness and the American Superhero." In *The Blacker the Ink: Constructions of Black Identity in Comics and Sequential Art*, edited by Frances K. Gateward and John Jennings, 137–152. New Brunswick, NJ: Rutgers University Press, 2015.

Frankenberg, Ruth. *White Women, Race Matters: The Social Construction of Whiteness*. London: Routledge, 1993.

Fredrickson, George M. *Racism: A Short History*. Princeton, NJ: Princeton University Press, 2002.

Fredrickson, George M. *White Supremacy: A Comparative Study in American and South African History*. New York: Oxford University Press, 1981.

Frye Jacobson, Matthew. *Roots Too: White Ethnic Revival in Post–Civil Rights America*. Cambridge, MA: Harvard University Press, 2008.

Fu, Albert S. "Fear of a Black Spider-Man: Racebending and the Colour-Line in Superhero (Re)Casting." *Journal of Graphic Novels and Comics* 6, no. 3 (July 3, 2015): 269–283.

Gallagher, Charles, and France Winddance Twine. "From Wave to Tsunami: The Growth of Third Wave Whiteness." *Ethnic and Racial Studies* 40, no. 9 (2017): 1598–1603.

Garner, Steve. *Whiteness: An Introduction*. London: Routledge, 2007.

Garvey, John, and Noel Ignatiev. "Abolish the White Race—by Any Means Necessary." *Race Traitor* 1, no. 1 (1993): 1–8.

Ghee, Kenneth. "'Will the "Real" Black Superheroes Please Stand Up?!': A Critical Analysis of the Mythological and Cultural Significance of Black Superheroes." In *Black Comics: Politics of Race and Representation*, edited by Sheena L. Howard and Ronald L. Jackson II, 223–237. London: Bloomsbury, 2013.

Glazer, Nathan, and Daniel P. Moynihan. *Beyond the Melting Pot: The Negroes, Puerto Ricans, Jews, Italians, and Irish of New York City*. Cambridge, MA: MIT Press, 1970.

Goldenberg, David M. *Black and Slave: The Origins and History of the Curse of Ham*. Berlin: Walter de Gruyter, 2017.

Grzanka, Patrick R., Keri A. Frantell, and Ruth E. Fassinger. "The White Racial Affect Scale (WRAS): A Measure of White Guilt, Shame, and Negation." *Counseling Psychologist* 48, no. 1 (January 2020): 47–77.

Guillou, Jan. "Tydligen är jag som vit en mindre önskvärd läsare." *Expressen*, October 11, 2020. https://www.aftonbldet.se/nyheter/kolumnister/a/0Kn38A/tydligen-ar-jag-som-vit-en-mindre-onskvard-lasare.

Harris, Cheryl L. "Whiteness as Property." *Harvard Law Review* 106, no. 9 (1993): 1707–1791.

Hassanein, Nada. "Native Americans Die Younger, CDC Study Shows. They Say It's Proof of 'Ongoing Systemic Harm.'" *USA Today*, November 23, 2021. https://eu.usatoday.com/story/news/health/2021/11/23/native-americans-life-expectancy-cdc/6360395001.

Hübinette, Tobias. *Att skriva om svenskheten: Studier i de svenska rasrelationerna speglade genom den icke-vita svenska litteraturen*. Malmö, Sweden: Arx förlag, 2019.

Hübinette, Tobias. "De icke-vita väljarna avgjorde det amerikanska presidentvalet och kan också komma att avgöra 2022 års svenska riksdagsval." *Tobias Hübinette*, November 14, 2020. https://tobiashubinette.wordpress.com/2020/11/14/de-icke-vita-valjarna-avgjorde-det-amerikanska-presidentvalet-och-kan-ocksa-komma-att-avgora-2022-ars-svenska-riksdagsval.

Hunt, Darnell, and Ana-Christina Ramón. "Hollywood Diversity Report 2020: A Tale of Two Hollywoods. Part 2: Television." Los Angeles: UCLA College of Social Sciences, 2020. https://socialsciences.ucla.edu/hollywood-diversity-report-2020.

Husain, Atiya. "Deracialization, Dissent, and Terrorism in the FBI's Most Wanted Program." *Sociology of Race and Ethnicity* 7, no. 2 (2021): 208–225.

Isenberg, Nancy. *White Trash: The 400-Year Untold History of Class in America*. New York: Viking, 2016.

Jordan, Jamal. "Issa Rae and the New Rules of Black TV." *MIC*, June 10, 2021. https://www.mic.com/culture/issa-rae-cover-story-october-2021.

Karlsson, Mattias, and David Lång. "Intensifierat arbete mot svenskfient-lighet." *Riksdagen*, 2013. https://www.riksdagen.se/sv/webb-tv/video/motion /intensifierat-arbete-mot-svenskfientlighet_H102A353.

Kassam, Shelina. "Feminists as 'Saviors' of Muslim Women: The Tension be-tween Gender Equality and Religious Rights." *Bloomsbury Religion in North America* (2021).

Kendi, Ibram X. *How to Be an Antiracist*. London: Bodley Head, 2020.

Kimmel, Michael S. *Angry White Men: American Masculinity at the End of an Era*. New York: Nation Books, 2013.

Kolchin, Peter. "Whiteness Studies: The New History of Race in America." *Jour-nal of American History* 89, no. 1 (June 2002): 157–173.

Kühl, Stefan. *For the Betterment of the Race: The Rise and Fall of the International Movement for Eugenics and Racial Hygiene*. Translated by Lawrence Schofer. New York: Palgrave Macmillan, 2013.

Kuhn, Gabriel. *Liberating Sápmi: Indigenous Resistance in Europe's Far North*. Oakland, CA: PM Press, 2019.

Kundnani, Arun. "Radicalisation: The Journey of a Concept." *Race and Class* 54, no. 2 (October 2012): 3–25.

Kyeyune Backström, Valerie. "Om det är detta som krävs är det orimligt." *Ex-pressen*, October 3, 2020. https://www.expressen.se/kultur/bocker/om-det-ar -detta-som-kravs-ar-det-orimligt.

Labba, Elin Lena. *Herrarna satte oss hit: om tvångsförflyttningarna i Sverige*. Stockholm: Nordstedts, 2020.

Lane, David. "White Genocide Manifesto." davidlane1488.com, n.d. https:// web.archive.org/web/20191001213058/https://www.davidlane1488.com /whitegenocide.html.

Lappalainen, Paul. "Det blågula glashuset—strukturell diskriminering i Sverige." Stockholm: Statens offentliga utredningar, 2005.

Larrick, Nancy. "The All-White World of Children's Books." *Saturday Review*, 1965.

"Le manifeste des 100." *Le Monde*, November 1, 2020. https://manifestedes90 .wixsite.com/monsite.

LeVine, Mark. "Abolishing Whiteness Has Never Been More Urgent." *Al Jazeera*, November 17, 2019. https://www.aljazeera.com/opinions/2019/11 /17/abolishing-whiteness-has-never-been-more-urgent.

Lindqvist, Sven. *The Dead Do Not Die: "Exterminate All the Brutes" and Terra Nullius*. Translated by Joan Tate and Sarah Death. New York: New Press, 2014.

Lipsitz, George. *The Possessive Investment in Whiteness: How White People Profit from Identity Politics*. 20th anniversary ed. Philadelphia: Temple University Press, 2018.

Lorde, Audre. *The Master's Tools Will Never Dismantle the Master's House*. Milton Keynes, UK: Penguin Books, 2017.

Lotz, Amanda Dyanne. "Segregated Sitcoms: Institutional Causes of Disparity among Black and White Comedy Images and Audiences." In *The Sitcom Reader: America View and Skewed*, edited by Mary M. Dalton and Laura R. Linder, 139–150. Albany: SUNY Press, 2005.

Lund, Martin. *Re-Constructing the Man of Steel: Superman 1938–1941, Jewish American History, and the Invention of the Jewish-Comics Connection*. New York: Palgrave Macmillan, 2016.

Lundström, Catrin, and Tobias Hübinette. *Vit melankoli: En analys av en nation i kris*. Göteborg, Sweden: Makadam förlag, 2020.

Macrooy, Jeangu. "I Know My Own Strength and That's What Will Keep Me Going"—the Netherlands' Jeangu Macrooy Discusses His Personal Connection to 'Birth of a New Age.'" Interview by Oliver Adams, April 26, 2021. https://wiwibloggs.com/2021/04/26/interview-netherlands-jeangu-macrooy -birth-of-a-new-age/264480.

Mbembe, Achille. *Critique of Black Reason*. Translated by Laurent Dubois. Durham, NC: Duke University Press, 2017.

McCormick, Andrew. "Madness on Capitol Hill." *Nation*, January 7, 2021. https://www.thenation.com/article/politics/capitol-trump-insurrection -explosions.

McGruder, Aaron. *A Right to Be Hostile: The Boondocks Treasury*. New York: Three Rivers Press, 2003.

McIntosh, Peggy. "White Privilege and Male Privilege: A Personal Account of Coming to See Correspondences through Women's Studies." Wellesley, MA: Wellesley College, Center for Research on Women, 1988. https://www .wcwonline.org/images/pdf/White_Privilege_and_Male_Privilege_Personal _Account-Peggy_McIntosh.pdf.

McIntyre, Alice. "Exploring Whiteness and Multicultural Education with Pro- spective Teachers." *Curriculum Inquiry* 32, no. 1 (2002): 31–49.

McMillan, Graeme. "Are American Comics Institutionally Racist?" *Gizmodo*, April 9, 2009. https://gizmodo.com/are-american-comics-institutionally-racist -5349421.

McMillen, Kristin, and Anna-Maria Carnhede. "SR tystar medarbetare som skrev under upprop mot rasism." *ETC*, February 2, 2021. https://www.etc.se /kultur-noje/sr-tystar-medarbetare-som-skrev-under-upprop-mot-rasism.

Mills, Charles W. *The Racial Contract*. Ithaca, NY: Cornell University Press, 1997.

Mir, Shabana. "How Not to Rescue Muslim Women." *Religion Dispatches*, April 16, 2009. https://religiondispatches.org/how-not-to-rescue-muslim-women.

Morrison, Toni. *Playing in the Dark: Whiteness and the Literary Imagination*. New York: Vintage Books, 1993.

Nuriddin, Ayah, Graham Mooney, and Alexandre I. R. White. "Reckoning with Histories of Medical Racism and Violence in the USA." *Lancet* 396, no. 10256 (October 3, 2020): 949–951.

Nygaard, Taylor, and Jorie Lagerwey. *Horrible White People: Gender, Genre, and Television's Precarious Whiteness*. New York: NYU Press, 2020.

Omi, Michael, and Howard Winant. *Racial Formation in the United States*. 3rd ed. New York: Routledge, 2015.

Orrenius, Niklas, and Barzan Dello. "Protestupprop mot rasism på Sveriges Radio i BLM-rörelsens spår." *Dagens Nyheter*, September 25, 2020. https://

www.dn.se/kultur/protestupprop-mot-rasism-pa-sveriges-radio-i-blm-rorel
sens-spar.

Oyola, Osvaldo. "Marked for Failure: Whiteness, Innocence, and Power in Defining Captain America." In *Unstable Masks: Whiteness and American Superhero Comics*, edited by Sean Guynes and Martin Lund, 19–37. Columbus: Ohio State University Press, 2020. http://public.eblib.com/choice/PublicFullRecord .aspx?p=6011669.

Oyola, Osvaldo. "'Say It Loud!' Tyroc and the Trajectory of the Black Superhero (Part 1)." *Middle Spaces* (blog), November 3, 2020. https://themiddlespaces .com/2020/11/03/say-it-loud-tyroc-pt1.

Painter, Nell Irvin. *The History of White People*. New York: W. W. Norton, 2011.

Pan, J. C. "Why Diversity Training Isn't Enough." *New Republic*, January 7, 2020. https://newrepublic.com/article/156032/diversity-training-isnt-enough -pamela-newkirk-robin-diangelo-books-reviews.

Pape, Robert A., and Chicago Project on Security and Threats. "Understanding American Domestic Terrorism: Mobilization Potential and Risk Factors of a New Threat Trajectory." Division of Social Sciences, University of Chicago, April 6, 2021. https://d3qi0qp55mx5f5.cloudfront.net/cpost/i/docs/americas _insurrectionists_online_2021_04_06.pdf?mtime=1617807009.

Prell, Riv-Ellen. *Fighting to Become Americans: Jews, Gender, and the Anxiety of Assimilation*. Boston: Beacon Press, 1999.

Prescod-Weinstein, Chanda. "Stop Equating 'Science' with Truth." *Slate*, August 9, 2017. https://slate.com/technology/2017/08/evolutionary-psychology-is -the-most-obvious-example-of-how-science-is-flawed.html.

Real, Michael, and Lauren Bratslavsky. "*The Cosby Show*: Recoding Ethnicity and Masculinity within the Television Text." In *The Sitcom Reader: America Re-Viewed, Still Skewed*, edited by Mary M. Dalton and Laura R. Linder, 149–164. Albany: SUNY Press, 2016.

Reese, Debbie. "An Indigenous Critique of Whiteness in Children's Literature." *Children and Libraries* 17, no. 3 (August 30, 2019): 3–11.

Rieber, John Ney, Chuck Austen, John Cassaday, Trevor Hairsine, and Jae Lee. *Captain America: Marvel Knights. Vol. 1*. New York: Marvel, 2016.

Roberts, Dorothy. "White Privilege and the Biopolitics of Race." *Understanding and Dismantling Privilege* 1, no. 1 (2010): 1–16.

Rockler, Naomi R. "*Friends*, Judaism, and the Holiday Armadillo: Mapping a Rhetoric of Postidentity Politics." *Communication Theory* 16 (2006): 453–473.

Roediger, David. "On the Defensive: Navigating White Advantage and White Fragility." *Los Angeles Review of Books*, September 6, 2018. https://lareviewof books.org/article/on-the-defensive-navigating-white-advantage-and-white -fragility.

Roediger, David. *The Sinking Middle Class: A Political History*. New York: O/R Books, 2020.

Roediger, David R. *Towards the Abolition of Whiteness: Essays on Race, Politics, and Working Class History*. London: Verso, 1994.

Roediger, David R. *Working toward Whiteness: How America's Immigrants Became White. The Strange Journey from Ellis Island to the Suburbs*. New York: Basic Books, 2005.

Röstlund, Lisa, and Erik Wikman. "Chatten avslöjar: Rasism, sexism—och krossade hjärtan." *Soldiers of Odin inifrån*. https://soldiersofodin.story.afton bladet.se/chapter/rasism-och-sexism.

Saini, Angela. *Superior: The Return of Race Science*. London: 4th Estate, 2020.

Schmidt, Jennifer M., and Mary West. "Whiteness Studies in South African Literature: A Bibliography." *English in Africa* 37, no. 1 (2010): 103–114.

Sguazzin, Antony. "South Africa Wealth Gap Unchanged Since Apartheid, Says World Inequality Lab." *TIME*, August 5, 2021. https://time.com/6087699 /south-africa-wealth-gap-unchanged-since-apartheid.

Shand-Baptiste, Kuba. "Opinion: The Government Is Not Taking Racism Seriously and Uses MPs of Colour to Avoid Criticism." *Independent*, October 22, 2020. https://www.independent.co.uk/voices/critical-race-theory-racism-kemi -badenoch-black-history-month-bame-discrimination-b1227367.html.

Singer, Marc. "'Black Skins' and White Masks: Comic Books and the Secret of Race." *African American Review* 36, no. 1 (2002): 107–119.

Smith, Kyle. "The White-Guilt Cult: A Look at Woke Religiosity." *New Republic*, June 18, 2020. https://www.nationalreview.com/magazine/2020/07/06 /the-white-guilt-cult/#slide-1.

Solomon, Akiba, and Kenrya Rankin, eds. *How We Fight White Supremacy: A Field Guide to Black Resistance*. New York: Nation Books, 2019.

Srinivas, Siri. "Super Sikh: A Superhero in a Turban Fighting Injustice and Ignorance." *Guardian*, March 9, 2015. https://www.theguardian.com/books/2015/mar/09/super-sikh-comic-book-superhero.

Steele, Shelby. "White Guilt." *American Scholar* 59, no. 4 (1990): 497–506.

Suhonen, Daniel, Göran Therborn, and Jesper Weithz, eds. *Klass i Sverige: Ojämlikheten, makten och politiken i det 21:a århundradet*. Lund, Sweden: Arkiv Förlag/Katalys, 2021.

Svenska barnboksinstitutet. "Bokprovning på svenska barnboksinstitutet: en dokumentation." Stockholm: Svenska barnboksinstitutet, 2019.

Takaki, Ronald T. *A Different Mirror: A History of Multicultural America*. New York: Little, Brown and Company, 2008.

Tännsjö, Torbjörn. "Det är inte fel att vilja ha perfekta människor." *Aftonbladet*, October 23, 2009. https://www.aftonbladet.se/a/4dEwLG.

Telles, Edward, and René Flores. "Not Just Color: Whiteness, Nation, and Status in Latin America." *Hispanic American Historical Review* 93, no. 3 (2013): 411–449.

Thomas, Ebony Elizabeth. *The Dark Fantastic: Race and the Imagination from Harry Potter to the Hunger Games*. New York: NYU Press, 2019.

Vandala. "'I Try to Keep Punk Rock Punk. You're Not Getting a Nice Story out of Me.' The Fat Mike Interview." *Vandala* (blog), January 3, 2017. https://vandalamagazine.com/2017/01/03/i-try-to-keep-punk-rock-punk-youre-not-getting-a-nice-story-out-of-me-the-fat-mike-interview.

Vergara, Daniel. "Nytt SD-initiativ—'Förenar dem med vit makt-miljön.'" Expo.se, November 2, 2020. https://expo.se/2020/11/nytt-sd-initiativ-%E2%80%9Df%C3%B6renar-dem-med-vit-makt-milj%C3%B6n%E2%80%9D.

Walt, Clint van der, Vijé Franchi, and Garth Stevens. "The South African Truth and Reconciliation Commission: 'Race,' Historical Compromise and Transitional Democracy." *International Journal of Intercultural Relations* 27, no. 2 (March 2003): 251–267. https://doi.org/10.1016/S0147-1767(02)00089-5.

Ware, Vron. *Beyond the Pale: White Women, Racism, and History*. New ed. London: Verso, 2015.

Watson, Veronica T. *The Souls of White Folk: African American Writers Theorize Whiteness*. Jackson: University Press of Mississippi, 2013.

Wekker, Gloria. *White Innocence: Paradoxes of Colonialism and Race*. Durham, NC: Duke University Press, 2016.

Welch, Brynn F. "The Pervasive Whiteness of Children's Literature: Collective Harms and Consumer Obligations." *Social Theory and Practice* 42, no. 2 (2016): 367–388.

Wikström, Peter, and Tobias Hübinette. "Equality Data as Immoral Race Politics: A Case Study of Liberal, Colour-Blind, and Antiracialist Opposition to Equality Data in Sweden." *British Journal of Social Psychology* (2021): 1–23.

Williams, Elizabeth M.. *The Politics of Race in Britain and South Africa: Black British Solidarity and the Anti-Apartheid Struggle*. London: I. B. Tauris, 2015.

World Health Organization. "Mercury in Skin Lightening Products." Geneva: World Health Organization, 2019. https://www.who.int/publications/i/item/WHO-CED-PHE-EPE-19.13.

Yang, Jeff, Parry Shen, Keith Chow, and Jerry Ma, eds. *Secret Identities: The Asian American Superhero Anthology*. New York: New Press, 2009.

FURTHER READING

Arvin, Maile. *Possessing Polynesians: The Science of Settler Colonial Whiteness in Hawai'i*. Durham, NC: Duke University Press, 2019.

Baldwin, James. *Notes of a Native Son*. London: Penguin Books Ltd., 2018.

Chow, Rey. *The Protestant Ethnic and the Spirit of Capitalism*. New York: Columbia University Press, 2002.

Du Bois, W. E. B. *Darkwater: Voices from within the Veil*. London: Verso, 2016.

Du Bois, W. E. B. *The Souls of Black Folk: Essays and Sketches*. New York: Fawcett Publications, Inc., 1961.

Dyson, Michael Eric. *Tears We Cannot Stop: A Sermon to White America*. Boston: Beacon Press, 2017.

Fanon, Frantz. *Black Skin, White Masks*. New York: Grove Press, 2008.

Fanon, Frantz. *The Wretched of the Earth*. New York: Grove Press, 2005.

Feagin, Joe R. *The White Racial Frame: Centuries of Racial Framing and Counter-Framing*. New York: Routledge, 2013.

Fields, Karen E., and Barbara Jeanne Fields. *Racecraft: The Soul of Inequality in American Life*. London: Verso, 2014.

Hamad, Ruby. *White Tears/Brown Scars: How White Feminism Betrays Women of Color*. London: Hachette, 2019.

Hübinette, Tobias. *Ras och vithet: svenska rasrelationer i går och i dag*. Lund, Sweden: Studentlitteratur, 2017.

Jackson, Lauren Michele. *White Negro: When Cornrows Were in Vogues . . . and Other Thoughts on Cultural Appropriation*. New York: Beacon Press, 2019.

Jordina, Ashley. *White Identity Politics*. Cambridge: Cambridge University Press, 2019.

Joshi, Khyati Y. *White Christian Privilege: The Illusion of Religious Equality in America*. New York: NYU Press, 2020.

Kindinger, Evangelina, and Mark Schmitt, eds. *The Intersections of Whiteness*. London: Routledge, 2019.

López, Alfred J. *Postcolonial Whiteness: A Critical Reader on Race and Empire*. Albany: SUNY Press, 2005.

Lundström, C. *White Migrations: Gender, Whiteness and Privilege in Transnational Migration*. London: Palgrave Macmillan, 2014.

Masuzawa, Tomoko. *The Invention of World Religions*. Chicago: University of Chicago Press, 2005.

Mbembe, Achille. *Necropolitics*. Translated by Steve Corcoran. Durham, NC: Duke University Press, 2019.

Melamed, Jodi. *Represent and Destroy: Rationalizing Violence in the New Racial Capitalism*. Minneapolis: University of Minnesota Press, 2011.

Mills, Charles W. *Black Rights/White Wrongs: The Critique of Racial Liberalism*. Oxford: Oxford University Press, 2017.

Oliver, Melvin, and Thomas M. Shapiro. *Black Wealth/White Wealth: A New Perspective on Racial Inequality*. New York: Routledge, 2006.

Olou, Ijeoma. *Mediocre: The Dangerous Legacy of White Male America*. New York: Hachette Book Group, 2020.

Picca, Leslie Houts, and Joe R. Feagin. *Two-Faced Racism: Whites in the Backstage and Frontstage*. New York: Routledge, 2007.

Rodney, Walter. *How Europe Underdeveloped Africa*. London: Verso Books, 2018.

Stokes, Mason. *The Color of Sex: Whiteness, Heterosexuality, and the Fictions of White Supremacy*. Durham, NC: Duke University Press, 2001.

Tehranian, John. *Whitewashed: America's Invisible Middle Eastern Minority*. New York: NYU Press, 2008.

Yancy, George, ed. *White Self-Criticality beyond Anti-Racism*. Lanham, MD: Lexington Books, 2014.

Zuberi, Tukufu, and Eduardo Bonilla-Silva, eds. *White Logic, White Methods: Racism and Methodology*. Lanham, MD: Rowman and Littlefield, 2008.

INDEX

MARTIN LUND is a senior lecturer in religious studies at Malmö University in Sweden.

CONTENTS

SERIES FOREWORD

The MIT Press Essential Knowledge series offers accessible, concise, beautifully produced pocket-size books on topics of current interest. Written by leading thinkers, the books in this series deliver expert overviews of subjects that range from the cultural and the historical to the scientific and the technical.

In today's era of instant information gratification, we have ready access to opinions, rationalizations, and superficial descriptions. Much harder to come by is the foundational knowledge that informs a principled understanding of the world. Essential Knowledge books fill that need. Synthesizing specialized subject matter for nonspecialists and engaging critical topics through fundamentals, each of these compact volumes offers readers a point of access to complex ideas.

INTRODUCTION

This book was written at a rare time. In summer 2020, global white public discourse came close to acknowledging that the workings of what some of us call whiteness is essential knowledge. Following the mass protests against police brutality and white supremacy that arose after the murder of George Floyd in Minneapolis, Minnesota, on May 25, 2020, and the backlash against them, whiteness briefly became a topic of white public concern. Demonstrations in solidarity with oppressed Black US Americans took place in many other countries, often in protesting police brutality, systemic racism, and white supremacy in those contexts too.[1] Movements were born, organizations were formed, solidarity was proclaimed, and books were sold. Some white people were talking about whiteness.

Even before the waves of protest rippled across the globe, the COVID-19 pandemic had convinced some white people who hadn't thought much about it before that their social, cultural, political, and economic position might privilege them with forms of defense against as well as concern about vulnerability that weren't extended to many others. And when anti-Asian violence and racism grew even more pronounced during the COVID-19 pandemic, a Stop Asian Hate movement emerged, leading to more discussions in white spaces about white people's role in the marginalization and oppression of people of Asian heritage in many countries. Some white people were thinking about whiteness.

This wasn't unprecedented. The civil rights protests in the 1950s' and 1960s' United States attracted an international white gaze that could not help but focus on whiteness. International white outcry over South African apartheid in the latter half of the 1900s couldn't ignore the centrality of whiteness to that oppression.[2] Once the protest and opposition subsided, however, whiteness quickly receded from the international consciousness. The pattern is familiar. From the vantage point of mid-2021, it seems like it's happening again. Many white people are forgetting about whiteness.

This book is about whiteness, written for people who want to learn why it is important to keep talking about whiteness, keep thinking about whiteness, and not forget whiteness once it is no longer spotlighted in white public forums. It's about how whiteness is more than what we sometimes see in the news. It's about an underlying cause of many global and local inequalities. It's about how what some of us call whiteness is created to begin with, how it changes, and how it serves to protect and privilege people who think we are white, or who are thought of as being white.[3] As such, it needs to begin with a question: Just what the hell does "whiteness" mean?

Whiteness 101

The introduction hedges a bit. It speaks about "what some of us *call* whiteness" and "people who *think* we are white." These phrasings should be thought of as implicitly permeating the rest of the book. They point to something central to any discussion of whiteness: whiteness doesn't exist, and there are no white people. Not really. Only people who are racialized as white. Rather, the point of departure for this book is that what some of us call whiteness is a racial formation that functions as a system of social control.

This definition will be unpacked more in the next chapter. For now it's enough to say that whiteness, as a racial designator, isn't a biological determinant of who and what people are but instead a social construction. Whiteness is not a quantifiable and inflexible fact of life, and not a scientific measure. Race, more than anything else, is about "making up people." Thus like any word used to describe a so-called race of people, "whiteness" only becomes meaningful in a social setting: it's defined, interpreted, and categorized in historical and cultural contexts. The word "whiteness" doesn't describe; it conjures into being. Whiteness is continually manufactured and sustained through language, laws, policies, science, representations in the news or popular culture and other media, and other channels. It is shaped and reshaped over time, through other ways of defining, interpreting, and categorizing who or what is to be thought of as white.

In this book, whiteness is not one single "thing" but rather a shifting master category. The term "whiteness" here designates a flexible cluster of historically, culturally, and geographically contingent ideals and standards. Whiteness isn't primarily about skin color or phenotype. After all, so-called white people aren't actually *white*. When I speak about whiteness, I speak about a system (or systems) of hierarchical classifications of race, class, gender, sexuality, physical ability, cultural capital, mental, cognitive, and intellectual capabilities, and other fluid aspects of identity. Whiteness rhetorically dissolves social differences and fosters the illusion among people who are called white that we have more in common with each other than we do with anyone else.[4]

In thinking about whiteness, we cannot avoid thinking about norms. Norms are socially constructed expectations, rules, patterns of behavior, and values that are

"Whiteness" only becomes meaningful in a social setting: it's defined, interpreted, and categorized in historical and cultural contexts. The word "whiteness" doesn't describe; it conjures into being.

upheld socially. Norms are artificial, but they are often treated as if they are not. In large parts of the world, whiteness is positioned as the normative, normalized, supposedly neutral or natural subject position—the universal baseline for human experience—from which "difference" and "deviance" are measured. This means that in a sense, whiteness is also obscured to those who are counted as white. This relationship can be considered through the theoretical construct of "figure" and "ground." In societies where whiteness is a dominant category, it can be viewed as the taken-for-granted ground on which, and in relation to which, other identity categories are given salience or figured.

One common way of framing this idea is to talk about the "invisibility" or "unmarkedness" of whiteness, even if it is not invisible as such. As media and cultural studies scholar and artist John Jennings points out, for example, "Growing up black, poor, and Southern made sure of my imperceptibility to the mainstream" in a world where the images available for consumption and self-creation were white.[5] It is never rare or odd for white people to see white people in cultural products like films or books, or on TV, notes author Reni Eddo-Ledge: "The positive affirmations are so widespread that the average white person doesn't even notice them. . . . To be white is to be human; to be white is universal. I only know this because I am not."[6] Whiteness is frequently all too visible to people of color, who generally must understand it in order to navigate societies organized for white people and against those figured as nonwhite. But because whiteness is often positioned as normative, and although it is sometimes mobilized when it can lead to (for whites) desirable ends, it is more difficult to perceive for those who are racialized as white. Whiteness doesn't usually come into white people's field of vision because it is the bifocal, binocular, or whatever other suitable metaphoric ocular device through which we perceive the world. This is a result of what sociology professor Eduardo Bonilla-Silva calls "white habitus": "a racialized, uninterrupted socialization process that *conditions* and *creates* whites' racial taste, perceptions, feelings, and emotions and their views on racial matters."[7]

When differential relations exist between groups, advantaged groups often develop their own "groupthink," Bonilla-Silva continues—that is, their own values and norms to account for those differences.[8] It follows that the greater the divergence from the ground—the dominant white norm in any given place and time—the more a group or person is figured to be different. This relation is made overly explicit in sociologist Nathan Glazer and politician and sociologist Daniel Moynihan's *Beyond the Melting Pot: The Negroes, Puerto Ricans, Jews, Italians, and Irish of New York City*. While the authors' introduction claims that there is "no great significance" to the order of the book's chapters, it is difficult to credit their claim when the next sentence sets up what appears to be a joke that hinges on racialized difference: "We begin, as the visitor might, with what immediately strikes the eye, and proceed from there." Turning the page, what "strikes the eye" is the chapter heading: "The Negroes."[9]

One benefit of the naturalization of whiteness is that it allows subjects to view themselves and be viewed as individuals first, rather than as member of groups. This is generally not a courtesy extended to those not considered white. Glazer and Moynihan's book has no chapter about the "whites of New York." That doesn't mean that whiteness is static or monolithic. As the next chapter shows, the borders are always fluid. The boundaries of whiteness in different national or regional contexts continuously shift to admit or reject certain groups to maintain the structures of privilege and marginalization. Whiteness is also relational. It cannot exist without something, or several somethings, figured as nonwhite. Sociologist Tressie McMillan Cottom summarizes these two points:

> Whiteness, the idea, the identity tethered in no nation of origin, no place, no gods, exists only if it can expand enough to defend its position over every group that challenges the throne. White is being European until it needs to also be Irish because of the Polish who can eventually be white if it means that Koreans cannot. For that situational dominance

to reproduce itself, there must be a steady pole. That pole is blackness.[10]

The history of whiteness in the United States is replete with examples of not-quite-white groups using the existence of Black people as a "stepping-stone" into whiteness, pointing out to the cultural center that "whatever else we may be, we're not Black." Similar stories have played out elsewhere, with some being whitened by the emergence or entrance of other, ostensibly less white groupings in the national demographics. Still, being figured as not white isn't the same as being figured as Black. While Islamophobia and anti-immigrant xenophobia directed at people of Middle Eastern–North African heritage are both common in Sweden, anti-Black or *afrofobiska* (Afrophobic) hate crimes are the most common form of hate crime, and many white Swedes continue to vocally defend the free use of the N-word whenever it is publicly debated. For that reason, and because the introductory genre necessarily must simplify, Blackness and whiteness function as the main "poles" in this book.

Whiteness also cannot be discussed without reference to racism. What racism means, however, is less straightforward than many of us think. One common and widely held definition of racism frames it as interpersonal, rooted in the belief that some groups are inherently different from and inferior or superior to others, and the individual attitudes, acts, and speech that follow from this belief. This book isn't primarily concerned with interpersonal racism but instead with racism as something structural, institutional, and systemic. Structural racism can be interpersonal in expression, but it is also, and more important, embedded in social, cultural, financial, and political institutions as well as norms, habits, stereotypes, prejudices, conventions, and practices. These aspects and others undergird a racial power structure that puts one group at a particular advantage while disadvantaging other groups. Structural racism doesn't require an ideology or particular attitude to be upheld as long as it's taken for granted. It's also impossible to opt out of a racist structure. It permeates every aspect of social life, affecting everybody whether we want it to or not. Being white—that is, being positioned as "white" according to a society's formations of "race"—does not mean that one is racist in the interpersonal sense. But it does mean that one is the beneficiary of a racist social order to some extent.

There is not, nor has there ever been, a singular "white" group. Who fits the description isn't uniform across time and space, and is contested across geography in any given era. Whiteness, then, is not so much about "white" bodies as it is about power. The critical term "whiteness" has been slowly emerging over the span of nearly two centuries as a focal point for discussion and activism in large part due to the work of people of color, especially Black US Americans for much of this time. With each passing year, more ways of talking about, thinking about, and remembering the shifting construction of whiteness appear, making it easier to critique, oppose, and perhaps eventually dismantle the global, regional, and local social orders that privilege whiteness as well as effect social control along racial lines.

Briefly about This Book

Whiteness is intended to serve as a way into a critical understanding of whiteness. As an introduction, it summarizes and synthesizes existing writing, and should not be viewed as a replacement for reading other work. A few words about the framing and limits of this book are thus in order. I write much about the cultural aspects of whiteness, but whiteness is always a project of racial domination. The ideas attached to whiteness have concrete effects. Those ideas are apprehended through representations. Representations help uphold domination and its effects. I discuss both structure and representation because they need each other to exist. Similarly, while I sometimes speak of whiteness in terms of knowledge, knowledge and ignorance about whiteness are always a matter of power. Ignorance isn't primarily an individual phenomenon; it's epistemic.

Whiteness is not
so much about
"white" bodies as it
is about power.